AIKIDO
in Everyday Life

AIKIDO
in Everyday Life
Giving in to Get Your Way

Terry Dobson
and
Victor Miller

North Atlantic Books
Berkeley, California

Cover photograph by Jan Watson
Cover design by Paula Morrison

 North Atlantic Books
P.O. Box 12327
Berkeley, California 94701

ISBN 1-55643-151-1

Aikido in Everyday Life: Giving in to Get Your Way is sponsored by the Society for the Study of Native Arts and Sciences, a nonprofit educational corporation whose goals are to develop an educational and crosscultural perspective linking various scientific, social, and artistic fields; to nurture a holistic view of arts, sciences, humanities, and healing; and to publish and distribute literature on the relationship of mind, body, and nature.

2 3 4 5 6 7 8 9 / 97 96 95 94 93

Dedicated to the memory of
MORIHEI UESHIBA

Contents

Preface to the Second Edition

In 1977, when this book was written, strut and muscle were "in" in the United States. Books titled *Winning Through Intimidation* and *Taking Care of Number One* topped the best-seller lists, and IBM's chest-thumping slogan for their salespeople was "It's hard to be humble when you know you're the best!" The art of Aikido was virtually unknown outside of Japan, and the idea that precepts deriving from a martial art (much less a martial art devoted to peace) could illuminate the conduct of one's daily affairs was too radical a notion for most publishers to consider seriously. Add to that Aikido's insistence on responsibility for the protection of one's adversary and it seems an absolute miracle the book got published when it did.

As it was, the publisher had a number of "considerations." For example, if we were going to espouse such far-out attitudes as *the restoration of harmony is the goal of all conflict and the best "victory" is the one in which everyone wins* then, by God, we would do it systematically. "Systems" were a big deal in those days, and Aikido was not. We were told to come up with a system. This requirement caused me great concern. Morihei Ueshiba had created this incomparable model of conflict resolution. Who was I to come along and try to shoehorn the principles he had so laboriously uncovered into a "system" to please somebody else? Then I remembered the many times O-Sensei had encouraged me to write about Aikido. "You must explain to the people of your country what you have learned by my side," he would say, "You must do your best to spread non-violence." So, with that as our rubric, Victor Miller and I sat down and worked out the "Attack-tics System." The publisher liked "Attack-tics"—the word had a tight, no-nonsense ring to it, just the thing to off-set the blue-sky babble about "harmony" and "confluence." Now, sixteen years later, "Attack-tics" is unknown and Aikido is a household word. It is as it should be. Still, the spirit of the book is true, its premises are sound, and I feel it should be republished. The reader is asked to excuse the outdated tone of the book—the attempt to be timely—and penetrate to the intent of the words. The feedback from the first printing has shown me that these words have changed lives for the better —perhaps they can change yours.

Terry Dobson
Vermont, 1992

Introduction

It would be relatively easy to write a book about harmony, singing the praises of cooperation and talking about the marvels of pacifism. We could all soothe one another and be thankful that conflict had been banished from our lives. No more squabbles with our children about going to bed, no more rages at the person who squeezes ahead of us in line, no more arguments with our friends about who did what to whom and why. In the blink of an eye we'd transform our existences into idyllic frolics on some pearl-white beach, attended by adoring friends who want nothing more than to share our peace and tranquility. (If we were travel agents and knew where this fantasy picture could be realized, we wouldn't have to write a book at all.)

But our lives are not like that. No one's is, regardless of social standing, financial leverage, or talent. Every day brings us painful conflicts, and there are days when we are the architects of other people's conflicts. We scold our children when they refuse to eat dinner, we swear at the other driver who claims he had the right of way, our bosses yell at us because they're mad at somebody else, we tell our wives or husbands they did this and that wrong, the cop claims the light was red, not yellow, and by the time we're ready to pack it in for bed, we're fighting our own selves about smoking, drinking, being stupid, being lazy . . .

Some days we're perfectly justified in saying that it's all too much, or, like Matthew Arnold in "Dover Beach":

> *And we are here as on a darkling plain*
> *Swept with confused alarms of struggle and flight*
> *Where ignorant armies clash by night. . . .*

We yearn for that elusive harmony, that peaceful beach. Unable to find it, we think there must be something wrong with us, and so off we troop to our psychoanalytic couches, self-help emporia, or instant-acting cure-alls. We drink a bit too much to blunt the pain of conflict. Or, if the pain becomes too great, we end it all.

All this tension about conflict is not really our fault, because we've never been told three very important things: One, conflict is neither bad nor good, it simply is; two, conflict is absolutely necessary to almost every life process; three, people need training in how to respond effectively and appropriately to conflict situations. For far far too long we've had a single view of conflict: that it is bad and that it demands a winner and a loser. Now, nobody would be foolish enough to suggest that people be taught how to engage in something bad, yet we do teach ourselves and our children, providing we are sufficiently motivated, how to execute a left jab, an uppercut, a karate chop. Even then we feel a vague sense of guilt or anxiety about somehow sanctioning conflict.

What we need is a new definition of conflict, a new way of looking at it, a new way of experiencing it, and a new way of responding to it.

Attack-tics offers us two things: a better way of viewing our daily struggles and a more effective way of handling them. On the way there, we will try to redefine winning and losing, moving away from the traditional "poker game" mentality toward a structure that will maximize everyone's potential. There are no losers in Attack-tics.

The route by which we arrived at this unique view and process was in itself unique. Attack-tics is the result of a wedding of the martial arts and theater—in this case, one very special martial art, Aikido, and one little-known aspect of theater, the rehearsal and training process. The two came together in the form of Terry Dobson, a teacher of Aikido, and Victor Miller, a teacher of theater games. The result, Attack-tics, uses the physical throws and body movements of Aikido as metaphors for the way in which to handle all forms of social or psychological attack.

Aikido, in its most formal manifestation, was the discovery of Morihei Ueshiba, a Japanese who at a very young age set out on the road to becoming the most ferocious martial artist in Japan. His motivation was quite simple. He had seen his father brutally assaulted by a gang of thugs, and resolved that he would never again be helpless. He reasoned that he could have come to his father's aid if only he had known how to fight.

In a relatively short time, Ueshiba had outstripped his masters in several of the martial arts. Acknowledged as the leading exponent of the way of the warrior, he should have settled down to teach, grow old, and make wise pronouncements. Fortunately, Ueshiba was troubled. With advancing age, he realized that his powers and prowess were deserting him. He saw that all his training, all his knowledge, was founded upon the principle of physical strength. He could hit harder, move faster, and dodge better than his opponents. But for how long? Like the aging gunfighter in American Westerns, Ueshiba was a ripe target for every younger, faster, stronger warrior who came along.

Mystical revelations do not necessarily occur on mountaintops. Ueshiba's revelation came to him while he was dumping a bucket of cold water over himself after a long, hot journey. "It was as if suddenly I could see everything clearly," he said. He realized that he, along with all the rest of us, had been sold a bill of goods—told that big is better than small, strong is better than weak, and quick is better than slow. From the very beginning we are taught that strength is physical.

It isn't.

Strength has more to do with intention than with the size of your biceps. It has more to do with your spirit and your energy flow than with the number of push-ups you can do. Aikido is the distillation of Ueshiba's vision and appreciation of what actually happens in nature. In hundreds of dojos (practice halls) across the world, Aikidoists are daily proving that a unified intention can accept and redirect the most awesome brute strength. It may be hard to accept, but it is a fact that a single reed can pierce a solid oak when blown with the force of a typhoon. You need only think of this image to appreciate the strength of a unified intention.

"Aikido," loosely translated, means a harmony of spirit and body, the opposite of what most of us experience when faced with conflict. It requires that the participant be "centered," relaxed, and alert. Moreover, Aikido is primarily a form of self-defense; it does not teach you how to run right out and break the nearest arm. Likewise, Attack-tics will not teach you how to *start* conflicts. The balanced person rarely feels the need to cause trouble.

We should bear in mind, finally, that Aikido (and, by extension, Attack-tics) is not a series of techniques for warding off disaster. It may begin that way, but you will quickly find that the more you practice the techniques and principles in this book, the more ingrained they will become, until they are simply part of a whole new outlook on conflict in interpersonal relationships, and a whole new outlook on life.

Now, where does the element of theater join with martial arts? For years theater games have been vehicles for teachers and actors and directors to explore the dynamics of human relationships on stage. In our Attack-tics workshops and training seminars we have borrowed these exercises in order to discover alternative methods for handling interpersonal conflict. In short, we improvise conflict situations with our clients so that they can practice their new behaviors in a low-risk setting. Some of the games and exercises are included in this book to give you the same opportunity.

What we hope you will take away from your reading and practice of Attack-tics is a new sense of power—the power that comes from knowing you can handle conflict in a way that is positive, humane, and mature; that you never have to fight someone unless you choose to; that in most situations you and your opponent can remain friends; that you don't need to win in situations where even the winner is really a loser.

And so, paradoxically, we *are* writing a book about harmony. Our goal is to help you achieve balance and harmony through the resolution of conflict. Remember, however, that harmony is inextricably bound up with the conflict from which it sprang. You may never find that tranquil beach—after all, the sand upon which you lie is the result of the conflict of rock and water against rock—but you need not be afraid to face your struggles. "Growing up," as a wise person once said, "is not for sissies."

New York and Stratford
1977

PART 1

BEGINNING ATTACK-TICS

I

Losers Weepers

Conflict wouldn't be so bad if
it weren't for the losing.

—Anonymous

YOU LOSE!

You lose because your idea of winning-and-losing will keep
you losing until you change that idea.

You lose because, like most of us, you've been sold a bill
of goods about victory.

You lose because you've been living your life as if your
family, friends, and co-workers had just suited up for a game
and you were the Oakland Raiders' front line.

You lose because your sense of yourself has mistakenly
become bound up with your tally on a nonexistent scoreboard.

You lose because even when you win, sometimes it feels as
if you lost.

"Lose" is one of the most depressing words in our language. Try a few of these expressions on for size:

"I lost my girlfriend to the captain of the football team."
"I lost my wallet yesterday."
"We lost the Maxwell House account."
"She lost her husband."
"We lost by two touchdowns."
"I lost my life savings in the market."
"The hikers became lost in the dense forest."
"I'm at a total loss as to what to do."
"He lost his job last year."
"Finders keepers, losers weepers."

That is truly a gloomy array of sentiments. And yet there is nothing particularly negative about the word "lose." The word itself is harmless. It depends on what's lost. If you lose something you don't want, then the word takes on entirely different connotations:

"He finally lost his fear of dogs."
"They're so much in love they lost all track of time."
"Fred gets lost in his hobby; it helps him unwind."
"Patty looks great—she must have lost twenty pounds!"
"Let's lose the kid and go to the movies alone."

That's not such a bad list of *losings,* but we tend to use the word in its negative sense far more often—so often that the word is indeed frightening.

From the first moment of consciousness to the last, we're afraid of losing. As infants we worry that we'll lose our parents. As adolescents we worry about losing our friends. As young adults we fear the loss of our identities. In middle age we worry about losing our security, our loved ones, our lives. To make ourselves feel better, we laugh at famous losers in history (General Custer, Marie Antoinette, Richard Nixon) or regale ourselves with tales of the loser at the office, down the block, in the White House. We teach our children how to be "good losers," but in our hearts we're afraid that Vince Lombardi was right: "Show me a good loser and I'll show you a loser" and "Winning isn't everything; it's the only thing."

Ah, but then there's the flip side to losing, which is supposed to make it all worthwhile. Perhaps . . .

"You won the million-dollar lottery!"

"Our firm won the contract over the other seventeen bidders."

"The competition was tough, but you won the starting berth on the team."

"He's a natural-born winner."

"Everybody loves a winner."

"We won by a score of six–love, six–love."

"She won his heart."

"I think we won him over to our side."

"We won the war."

"She won the suit and was awarded half a million dollars in damages."

Just reading about winning is enough to cheer up most people. Winning is supposed to be everything that losing is not. The winner feels good about himself or herself. The winner has charisma; people hang around winners. Agencies and firms that land big contracts seem to reap even bigger contracts because everybody in the trade knows them as winners.

Well, we may do our utmost to keep them hidden, but just as there are positive aspects to losing, so are there negative aspects to winning.

There's the compulsion of the winner to keep on winning, the drive that results in more heart attacks per cubic inch of aorta than losing ever did. Thus, we wax poetic over the gold-medal winner who dies young, never having to face the diminution of his powers. We compile studies about how, ironically, winners are pushed by their admirers into their own eclipse: the bullfighter who is cheered into working too close to the horns; the actor who takes ridiculous roles just to keep himself before the public's critical eye.

For all that, we are a nation dedicated to winning, founded on the concept that any person can win, and baptized in the belief that there is something wrong with the loser.

The truth is, there's nothing wrong with winning.

Provided that what you are winning is a contest.

One more time: *There's nothing wrong with winning, provided that what you are winning is a contest.*

The problem which Attack-tics will address itself to is that, over the years, we've let the win/lose frame of reference shift into areas of our lives that are *not* contests. Tennis, football, hockey, and volleyball are contests; they have rules and scores. Sex, fame, love, appreciation, maturity, and child-raising (to name a few areas of human behavior) are not contests, do not have uniform rules, and never did have scores until we began keeping them.

There was a time, not too long ago, when the average bookstore browser could find half a dozen good books on football fundamentals and one book for adolescents on what sex was all about. Nowadays you go into a store and you find a dozen books on how to improve your copulatory skills— as if sex were somehow the same as punting, passing, and tackling! To be sure, there's nothing whatsoever wrong with being a better love partner. It's a glorious idea. What's happened, however, is that the emphasis on skills has not-so-subtly convinced would-be lovers that sex is a competitive contact sport—a contest. We can hear it now: "Okay, fans, our contender, that plucky little lover from New York, is down by six orgasms and he really has his work cut out for him . . ."

On a less lascivious level, consider the mother and son who've reached a Mexican standoff in the Bathtub game. The scoring is very simple: If he gets wet, he loses; if he stays dry, he wins. If she can get him to take a bath without employing physical violence, she's a good mommy and wins the Good Mommy game; if she has to call Daddy or spank the child, she goes to the bottom of the league standings. Just as with lovemaking, parenting has become an exercise of skill which too often calls for a winner (the parent) and a loser (the recalcitrant child, who identifies bathing with a twenty-touchdown loss).

How about the fight over the parking space? The other car cuts you off and you lose the Parking Space game. Or how about the woman who jams her shopping cart against your ankles? She is playing Supermarket, and you're afraid that if you let her get away with it the fans will boo you at the checkout counter. You're going to be traded down to the minor leagues, where you fear you belong.

So? So our lives are absolutely crammed with these mis-guided perceptions of life's events as some form of game— a game we're desperately afraid of losing.

If we don't kick back at the angry lover, we'll lose: "He won't respect me; he'll wipe the floor with me the next time!"

If we don't reprimand the back-talking secretary, we'll have lost: "She'll lose respect for me!"

If we don't put down the carping parent, he'll have won: "I worked too hard to gain his grudging respect to lose it now!"

You know why some days it seems as if everybody's winning but you? Because you've bought into an imaginary, arbitrary system where everything's a contest and there are no ties—just sudden-death play-offs and a long walk to the showers.

Nature, as we'll see in the next chapter, is full of conflict.

But, look around you. You won't find a scoreboard. Who, for example, is the winner in cell division? Who is the loser when wind and water clash to create an awe-inspiring wave? Are we winners or losers when gravity clamps down on us, forcing us to stay put?

Face it: You've been sold a bill of goods. It's normal to want to win, but you've been led to believe that you must win or lose every conflict in life, and that just isn't so.

The first step in Attack-tics is to stop seeing everything as a contest, which by definition must have a winner and a loser.

ZERO-SUM GAMES

Certainly there are many life conflicts where the dynamics *demand* a winner and a loser. Life is still full of what game theorists call "zero-sum games"—contests. In poker, for example, the total amount of money won and lost must add up to zero. You win five, I lose five—zero. Likewise, if Ted and Sam are in love with Marcia, there's only the slimmest chance that Marcia will accept both of them as husbands, either concurrently or consecutively. There's no way to "play" at love or poker so that everyone leaves the "game" happy.

In a sense, war also falls into the category of a zero-sum game. Rarely can you have a tie in a war. For example, it would have been morally reprehensible for the U.S. and the Allies to have "settled out of court" with the Third Reich, asking Hitler to annex only half of Holland and to slaughter only half its citizens. These are not the kinds of conflicts we're talking about.

So there's nothing inherently wrong with winning or losing. The important thing to keep in mind is that not all conflicts are contests. *Not every conflict is a zero-sum game,* which *requires* a winner and a loser. Each conflict does require a careful assessment of what's really going on.

HOW DOES IT FEEL?

Let's take a look at the pressure we put on ourselves to avoid being losers and the rewards we feel when we win some of life's non-contests. Imagine that you are "A" in the following scene. You've been on the job only a few months, working for "B," a hard man who would just as soon believe that no one can do the job right and that most people are incompetent. You're not feeling well this morning, haven't had your coffee yet, and the boss steps up to your desk. As the scene unfolds, try to catalogue your feelings—if A were really you.

B: Morning, A, I thought I'd stop by and have a chat with you.

A: Good morning, Mr. B. Anything wrong?

B: No, just the opposite.

A: What is it?

B: You know, I was not really in favor of hiring you in the first place.

A: I'd heard some rumors to that effect, sir.

B: And then, when you took on the XYZ account, I must admit I was worried about your competence.

A: I didn't know that.

B: But I just took a look at our fourth-quarter earnings on XYZ, and I'm here to tell you I was wrong and I'm man enough to admit it.

A: Thank you, sir. I did my best.

B: You were responsible for a net gain of thirty-two points over last quarter. You're a winner, A, and I'm putting you

in for a raise. I'd also like to talk to you about seeing if we
can't put you in a supervisory capacity on some of the
other accounts that are foundering.

A: Yessir!

Later C, D, and E come up to congratulate you. You go
home and celebrate. And you have every right to. You did
your best, and it got you a victory of real magnitude.

Make a list of the feelings you experienced during the
scene as A; or, if that is too abstract for you at the moment,
make a list of what you felt when *you* last won something,
when somebody told you you'd done a good job on a project.
Try to avoid words like "good" and "ecstatic" and instead
see if you can remember what your body felt like, what kinds
of things went through your mind, how you behaved. We're
interested in the sensations that go with your victories.

No two human beings feel precisely the same way in a
victory situation. One person might feel warmth spreading
through his chest; another is conscious of "watery" wrists;
another cries like a baby. One victor feels compelled to run
right out and buy something, while another feels the need to
get roaring drunk. The bottom line, quite obviously, is that
winners feel good.

Losers don't.

What does it feel like to lose?

Now see if you can identify with A in the following scene,
and again pay particular attention to how and what you feel.
It's the same office, same boss, same situation.

B: A, what the hell do you think you're up to?
A: Sir?
B: I asked you a simple question.
A: I don't understand.
B: That's for sure! You don't understand a goddamned thing!

Ever since we took you on—and you better believe I'm
going to ask Personnel why we did—you've been fouling
up everything you touch! What happened to the Ryan
contract?

A: My, uh, secretary hasn't been able to find it yet, sir.

B: You blaming her for the Towers screw-up too? Or losing
out on that Los Angeles deal?

A: I'm doing my best . . .

B: Tough. You're out. Fired!

And the word goes out on the jungle telegraph that A is a
loser.

Make a list of the feelings you experienced as A during this
scene. Again, if you'd rather, think back to the last time you
performed poorly and thought of yourself as a loser. Just as
with the first list, avoid general adjectives like "awful,"
"sad," "depressed." Ask yourself what your body felt like,
what kinds of things went through your mind, what behaviors you demonstrated. What kinds of sensations go along
with your defeats?

There's no single description of how it feels to lose. Some
people feel smaller in stature. Their shoulders round down
toward the ground and, quite literally, they *are* smaller.
Some get headaches; some become sleepy and try to escape
the reality by actually closing their eyes. Some weep, some
rage. All feel simply terrible about themselves. (If you're
having a hard time conjuring up the sensations, try remembering how you felt when you made a major purchase and
then found you could have bought the same item for forty
percent less at another store!)

Now put your two lists in front of you—the winner list
and the loser list. They represent, in brief, what is at
stake for you in any contest you engage in. One side is
the prize, the other the punishment. They are the *why* of

your fighting. They go a long way toward explaining the peaks and valleys of your life, the depressions and the euphorias. They are, in short, why you bought this book in the first place.

Nobody in his or her right mind wants to feel the sensations on your loser list. We would all like to feel—permanently—those on your winner list. Well, we're here to tell you that it's possible. Using the ATTACK-TICS System, you can emerge from conflict feeling positive, like a human being full of potential, capable of giving and receiving love. We don't promise you'll feel that way after a tennis match against Jimmy Connors, but you *can* experience those positive feelings after the really important non-contests with friends, lovers, fellow employees, people on the street.

Keep both lists posted where you can see them: above your desk, on your refrigerator, wherever you spend time, wherever you find yourself in conflict. Consult the loser list whenever you can. Be aware that if you persist in responding to conflict in the old way, this is how you will feel when you "lose." Remember also that when your opponent is forced to his knees, he'll feel much the same way. *That* is how you are making someone else feel. So, as we see it, either way you lose.

Attack-tics can make sure that both of you, the aggressor and the target of that aggression, end up with the feelings on your winner list. Just being aware of these two choices can help you refrain from creating contests where there are none and from trying to defeat people.

This perspective should help you get beyond the concept of winning and losing.

HAP AND BOB

If you can't find a way to get beyond the idea that all life is a contest, you're going to be fated to live it as Hap and Bob do, clinging rockbound to your scorecards.

Hap and Bob are best friends. They are both single. Moreover, they subscribe to an altogether counterproductive view loosely known as "male chauvinism." The seduction of women is, for them, only the first round in the Battle of the Sexes. They hate losing, at anything, and they've created hundreds of opportunities to test themselves.

Hap, feeling poorly about the way things are going at work, having lost out to a faster car at the traffic light, having been snubbed by the woman at the end of the bar, turns to Bob and makes an offhand comment about Bob's lack of success with women. Even his language is filled with sports metaphors: "Bob, old buddy, you haven't scored with a chick in a week. You're really striking out."

Up to this point, Bob has been feeling pretty good. But since there's more than a grain of truth in what Hap says, he perceives Hap's statement as an attack and is devastated by it. His forehead gets hot, his eyes narrow, his breath is constricted by a chest that's pounding, and his blood pressure rises dramatically. His mind rips through all its old file folders, trying to edit out all the misadventures he's had with women, racing on to find fault with Hap's "scorecard." Finally (in a split second, actually) he blurts out: "Oh yeah? How about the time you came on to Anne-Marie and she laughed right in your face!"

The tables are turned: Now it is Hap who is feeling attacked. The conflict has been joined, the battle has begun.

Hap and Bob spend the next two hours yelling about who's

had the most or fewest dates, affairs, etc. Worse than that, the fight—for that's what it has become—does not stop with the original topic, but escalates into other areas. By the time their friendship lies in tatters, Hap and Bob have accused each other of child-molestation, grand-theft auto, and devil worship.

Why? Because they perceived the conflict as a contest, a zero-sum game. Hap thinks he would have lost if he had said, "Yes, I really do need help in relating to women." As a loser he'd experience all those awful feelings you listed a few pages ago. Neither Hap nor Bob wants to feel bad about himself, so each struggles harder to keep from "losing."

But—and this is the important "but"—*who really wins?* Bob slams the door louder and feels he's won. Hap bloodies Bob's nose and feels *he's* won. Bob comes up with forty documented instances of Hap's awkwardness with women and *he's* won? And the dumbest part is that women aren't a game, and the fight is really about how Hap and Bob feel about themselves.

And the complications don't even stop there. Besides the fact that Hap is now short one friend, he's stuck with the problem of making sure that Bob knows that Hap won! He rushes to the phone to call a dozen of his friends and tells them in great detail about how he just devastated poor old Bob. That makes Hap feel better, because everybody he talks to tells him "Of course you were right. You're great with women." Hap also hopes that the word will get back to Bob, just to make things complete. Perhaps tomorrow one of their mutual acquaintances will sidle up to Bob and say, "Boy, I heard you really got whipped by Hap last night . . ."

It isn't enough that we know in our heart of hearts that we won a "fight"; we have to make sure our vanquished foes know, too! Of course, in a real game there's no question—the score tells it all. In these dangerous non-games we're talking about, the only "scores" are vague statements about "saving face," "getting our way," "not letting her get away with it," "showing somebody up," or, more modernly, "asserting ourselves."

Is it an act of "self-assertion" to rescue your child from a burning building? Hardly. You wouldn't say you "beat" the fire. Clearly, there is no contest here. And yet we're always edging ever closer to the brink of absurdity, saying and believing things like "I beat Mount Everest!" when that much-maligned piece of nature never even knew it was fighting anybody.

Getting back to Hap and Bob, we can identify one of the most counterproductive elements in the syndrome of imagined contests. Hap now sits at home, and, like most of us in these situations, he isn't very happy. He thinks that he knows that he won, but he's still not happy. He fought his best friend just so he wouldn't end up unhappy, and yet here he is feeling miserable. He's lost a friend, and he's not a bit proud of the way he conducted himself. He wishes he could retract that killer statement "I never really liked you, Bob!" Worse than losing the argument, Hap lost control.

And yet the whole purpose of the fight was love. After all, isn't love what lies behind the desire to win? "Everybody loves a winner." Those absurd daily "victories" in non-contests like Hap's are really our way of shopping for love. It would be too embarrassing to ask just for approval or love, so we do a little conquering here, a little conquering there, and by the end of the day we don't feel we're such bad eggs after all.

And that's what it's really all about: *self*-approval. Seeking the approval/love of everyone we meet is just seeking a substitute for the love we should be giving to ourselves. Most of us aren't strong enough in the ego department to walk out the door and take a moment to say, "I'm a dynamite person, able to love and worthy of it!" But we figure if Eddie, Francine, George, and a half million of our closest friends *see* us win and cheer us to victory, then we must be okay people.

Everybody wants approval and needs love. But the fastest way to fool yourself that you've gotten both is to win something by destroying somebody else in the process.

The purpose of Attack-tics is, in part, to get us all to be able to stand outside the arena of win-and-lose so that we can decide, as objectively as possible, what is really happening in the conflicts we face. If we can meet an angry friend or a recalcitrant child without worrying about wins and losses, we will immediately be better, more understanding, more effective parents, friends, and workers.

The point, of course, is that it's not whether you win or lose, but whether you *choose* to play the game!

II

Conflict

In the cold Northern wastes
There is a mountain
A thousand miles long
A thousand miles high

Once each thousand years
A small bird
Flies North
A small bird flies North
to sharpen his beak
on the cold hard stone

When the mountain
Is thusly worn down
One second of Eternity
Shall have passed.

—Tibetan poem

Conflict is necessary for all life.

You cannot escape it, and you shouldn't even want to.

Conflict is the opposition of wills, principles, or forces. It is part of our biology, our psychology, and our daily lives. It drives the music we listen to, the cars we drive, and it permits the birds to fly. Can you imagine a concerto without a conflict and a resolution? We'd end up listening to one unwavering note for forty-five minutes—no rests, no rhythm changes, no contrapuntals, just one note. And even then we'd have trouble hearing it if it were not for the opposition of the sound waves against our eardrums.

If we did away with all conflict overnight, we'd be in truly big trouble. Our cells would stop regenerating, but then there wouldn't be any wearing away of our bodies by time, age, weather, or stress, either. We couldn't oppose the inertia of a ten-penny nail, build a bridge or an arch for a cathedral. All the laws of thermodynamics would go right out the window, and the laws of motion would follow them.

Surfers would wonder where the waves had gone, because wind, water, and tide would all be in harmony. Sailors would have a hard time sailing, because the wind would constantly shift rather than oppose the sails that drive the boat. Actually, there would be no wind, thanks to static temperature across the globe.

We'd find it difficult to walk, because we'd always be balanced and walking is a process wherein balance is achieved, upset, and achieved again. Eating would be a tricky process at best, because our teeth would certainly not want to oppose one another in order to grind. Our uppers and lowers would harmonize and wind up side by side!

Okay, so that's impossible and ridiculous—but it's just as ridiculous to perceive conflict as something evil. It's fully time for us to see conflict as a function of nature instead of pretending that it's a punishment for Adam and Eve's misadventure with the apple. The plants in the Garden of Eden could not have yielded any fruit anyway, because it is the breaking apart and reforming of cells which constitutes growth.

So one of the first steps in the Attack-tics process is to accept conflict as part of the natural order of things. *Conflict simply is.* That doesn't mean we have to like it or enjoy it or cause it or seek it or get off on it. Attack-tics is not some new form of fascism; it is a vital form of protection which demands that conflict be understood and accepted for what it is. And understanding it means that a reasonable response to conflict is possible—unless we see all conflicts as equally threatening, we misperceive a conflict, or we don't even see it coming.

MAGNIFIERS: PEOPLE WHO SEE ALL CONFLICT AS EQUALLY THREATENING

Sad to say, there are people who see all conflicts as equal in importance. Inside their bodies or psyches or wherever such organs are hidden, they have a conflict-control center which has no throttle, just an off/on switch. They react as if the child with dirty hands is as much of a problem as the child who's playing with matches; as if the person who accuses them of gossiping is just as serious a threat as the person who swears to kill them.

In other words, the Magnifier goes *beyond* the immediate conflict, magnifying the situation beyond its true proportions. The child with dirty hands is certainly an esthetic threat, possibly even a hygienic threat, but in the immediate situation he is a threat, on a low level of priority, only to himself. The child with the matches may be as clean as a whistle, dressed in Eton collar and shiny Buster Browns, but he is a threat to everyone in the house as well as to himself. If only because of the number of potential victims involved, his conflict is on a higher level of priority.

Magnifiers have no sense of priority.

But it's so obvious, you say. Nobody could possibly equate being burned alive with being disgusted. Well, in our workshops we've had to deal with conflicts that were just as exaggerated. How about the office worker who perceives his desk-location change as a conflict equal to his being fired? Daily jobs are literally crammed with just such conflicts that are given higher priority than they deserve.

Remember: Each conflict must be viewed in terms of the importance you *consciously* assign to it. All conflicts are not equally threatening.

MISPERCEIVERS: PEOPLE WHO
MISPERCEIVE CONFLICT

Misperceiving conflict is just as dangerous as seeing all conflicts as equally threatening. It is also just as prevalent. Most characteristically, the Misperceiver makes one of two crucial errors: 1) He sees conflict where there is none; or, 2) he reads conflict incorrectly and fights about something other than what the fight is really about. The Misperceiver is the person who tends to turn every conflict into a win/lose situation. His framing mechanism, his way of interpreting what he sees, is in bad repair, and he needs to find a new perspective.

Let's first look at the Type 1 Misperceiver: the person who sees conflict where there is none. Bill is our chronic Misperceiver. He works for a large company, as does Jack, whose history would indicate that he's a pretty fair person. One day over lunch Jack says, "The boss said he's sick and tired of long memos." Now, Bill has always dreaded writing, because he has a difficult time making himself clear. He agonizes over everything that goes out over his signature. Because of this sore point, it's not unlikely that Bill perceives, through his limited frame of reference, that Jack has just attacked him. Criticized him. He might even go as far as to imagine that this is the boss's and Jack's way of telling him his writing is lousy. He has a neat mental image of Jack and the boss chuckling over his lengthy memos.

This makes Bill angry.

Before push and shove even come near each other, Bill turns to Jack and says, "Well, nobody outside of a loony bin could understand that garbage *you* write!"

"What's that supposed to mean?" Jack replies.

And the conflict is on.

To be sure, it *is* possible that Jack and the boss have singled out Bill as the writer of long memos. This could be the boss's way of getting the word to Bill, at a low risk level, without embarrassing him. But even so, what is there to fight about? Either Bill writes long memos or he doesn't, and if he does, can he convince anyone that his writing is brief? Whom does he want to convince, anyway? In short, Bill has forgotten to ask himself one of the most important questions in Chapter I: Is this a win/lose situation? The answer, of course, is *no*. Jack has made a statement. No matter how mean-spirited Jack may be, there is no contest here, and Bill would be far better off just tucking the information away for thought and future reference.

Instead, Bill chooses to misperceive the event as a contest called "I'm okay, and probably better than you." In doing so he forgets to examine an important operative element of the event: Jack's history. Nothing in Jack's previous behavior would lend credence to Bill's perceiving his statement as an attack. *Each conflict must be seen not only in the present context but also as a result of whatever has gone before.*

The second type of Misperceiver makes the mistake of reading incorrectly what an argument is really about. As a result, he wins the battle he's fighting but loses the fight he cannot see.

Sheila and Phil have been married for two years. They

have what their friends call a "combative relationship."
Some unnamed urge drives them to create win/lose situations over everything from who does the dishes to what will
happen in bed.

In the following instance, Sheila and Phil have just weath-
ered a fairly mediocre lovemaking experience. Sheila feels
unsatisfied, and Phil feels he's stuck with an unresponsive
partner. Sheila begins the first attack:

> SHEILA: Phil, I'm really angry at you for spending all that
> money on *your* new TV set.

Notice how clever Sheila is, concealing her feelings about
being unfulfilled by attacking Phil's spending. The TV now
stands for the gyp in bed she feels she's gotten from Phil.
Moreover, she's being "dishonest with honesty" by using the
frontal approach: "I'm really angry . . ." Since nowadays it's
honest and good and true to be direct with your feelings, she
comes on very strong as an up-front person. Unfortunately,
she's being up-front about the wrong thing.

Phil makes the mistake of responding to Sheila's stated
argument about the TV. If he were a better perceiver, he
would sense that she is upset about something else and try
to help her with that. Instead, he pounds his pillow with his
fist.

> PHIL: I don't spend as much money on luxuries as you do!
> How about that vanity-mirror thing?

Good for Phil! He's struck Sheila where she lives. He's
attacked her vanity as well as her overspending. Notice that
neither is any closer to what underlies the fight.

SHEILA: My mirror, which you use all the time, didn't cost half of what that monstrous-looking TV set cost!

She's playing the same game now, arguing point for point and counterattacking in the area of Phil's taste.

The battle goes on, both Phil and Sheila consciously or subconsciously misperceiving what the fight's really about. Phil finally wins—or thinks he does—by adding up all the purchases Sheila has made in the last two years and demonstrating irrefutably that he is less of a spendthrift.

Isn't that marvelous? Think of the anguish and energy that just went into a fight, a conflict, that was only a cover-up for what the fight was really about. But we keep on doing what Sheila and Phil did, don't we? Most often we do it because we really don't know what's troubling us. And sometimes we do it because we're afraid of what the real fight could be about.

These smokescreen fights will continue until the larger issue is defused in some way. Until that happens, the larger issue stays behind the scenes, energizing those petty battles.

Again, then, it's crucial that you know what each conflict is really about. You've got to ferret out the larger issue by examining what has just gone before and asking some pertinent questions: What else is bothering me and him or her? What else could this be about? What could I be hiding from? Is my emotion equal to the importance of the conflict, or am I overreacting for some reason? *What could that reason be?*

The next time you sense that your attacker is disguising the real issue, calmly ask "Is this what's really bothering you, or is there something else?" Our experience shows us that, at the very least, the attacker will stop dead in his or her tracks for a few seconds. The more reasonable, self-aware attacker will concede your point. The less self-aware will charge forward on the trivial point but without as much determination as before. And you will be able to congratulate yourself on having perceived a conflict correctly.

The Magnifiers and the Misperceivers are, for the most part, a scrappy lot of people who are known as fighters— sometimes in a positive sense, sometimes in a negative one. They probably do not "win" very often, even on their own terms. The next type is quite the opposite. He or she appears to have capitulated to life, and as a result misses a great deal of what is going on.

FAILED PERCEIVERS:
PEOPLE WHO DON'T SEE IT COMING

The Failed Perceiver is like the Misperceiver in that his frame of vision is equally faulty. However, the Failed Perceiver doesn't see the *wrong* conflict; he sees no conflict at all, even when he's right in the middle of it. He wears a specially constructed set of blinders and breezes along into oblivion.

Take Joanne, a relatively typical Failed Perceiver. She has two kinds of friends: those who like her because she never gets angry and those who are furious with her because she never gets angry. Her speech is filled with lines like "Well, I'm sure she didn't mean it that way," "There's nothing you can do about it."

Now, there's nothing wrong with being calm and understanding. Joanne's difficulty is that her calm and understanding are inappropriate responses to actual life events. She has bought off her involvement.

Take the times she deals with Angela, who, for reasons of her own, is always managing to say relatively unkind things to Joanne. "Are you putting on weight?" "Are you sure you look your best in blue?" "If I were you, I'd sue your hairdresser for malpractice." None of the attacks—and we know they're attacks because of Angela's history as well as the characteristic way she asks questions instead of making statements—is, in the ultimate scheme of things, earth-shattering. If Joanne never reacts at all, people will not starve and Joanne will not die at the hands of Angela. But Joanne has the right to go through life without having to put up with Angela's carping, and as Angela's friend she has the responsibility of setting her straight. Moreover, another problem with Failed Perceiving is that small, overlooked conflicts can sooner or later escalate into large, uncomfortable conflicts. This is because it is in the nature of attackers to keep on attacking until they get the response their own character structures demand. They won't dry up and go away—not until they are called on their behavior.

> ANGELA: Are you feeling all right?
> JOANNE: I'm fine.
> ANGELA: You look peaked.
> JOANNE: I feel okay, I guess.
> ANGELA: Maybe it's the color of your blouse. It gives your face a greenish tinge.
> JOANNE: I didn't know that.
> ANGELA: Which really doesn't go at all well with that skirt.
> JOANNE: Gee.
> ANGELA: Sometimes I think you've really got to be taken in hand. Where did you get your taste in clothes?
> JOANNE: I don't know. It just kind of happened.
> ANGELA: I'll say.

It may appear absurd on the printed page, but we've heard conversations similar to this one. Joanne begins by losing confidence in how she feels physically and ends up wondering if life is worth living at all. Angela just keeps on poking, making herself feel superior, and she'll continue poking until Joanne gets the message. Angela is *looking* for conflict, which is her way of making herself feel good. Until she gets the fight, she won't let up. Until she's been destructive, she won't quit.

And what are they going to fight about? Whether or not Joanne looks peaked? Whether or not her taste is awful? People fight for less. Every day . . .

The final problem with being a Failed Perceiver is that ultimately you get clobbered. You miss cue after cue and sign after sign until it's too late. For instance, in the Jack-and-Bill scenario a few pages back, Bill would have been even worse off if he had failed to perceive the conflict concerning the memos, for he would have gone right along writing the same old way and would have lost a chance to improve himself in his profession. Sometimes Failed Perceiving is worse than Misperceiving. A Misperceiver risks taking inappropriate action; a Failed Perceiver risks taking no action at all.

Remember: *It is important to perceive conflict where it exists.* If you follow these important rules, you cannot fail.

1) Take the past into consideration.

2) Be on the lookout for questions which are really statements. ("Are you sure you should be wearing yellow?" usually means "I don't think you should be wearing yellow!")

3) Observe the person's face (especially the eyes), manner, breathing, posture, etc.

4) Listen carefully to what is being said and, just as important, to what is *not* being said.

When dealing with conflicts:

1) Don't see all conflicts as equally threatening.

2) See conflicts for what they are, not for what they may appear to be.

3) See conflict if it is there.

You don't have to be paranoid or defensive, just awake and alert.

To sum up our exploration of conflict, then, we know that conflict is a constant, a given in nature, which has no intrinsic value system. Conflict is neither good nor bad; it simply is. Viewing it this way, you can begin to assess conflict with an eye toward responding more appropriately and more effectively.

III

There's More to Conflict than Fight or Flight

Conflict should always be so
managed as to remember that
the only true end of it is peace.

—Alexander Pope

As we have been saying all along, in any conflict situation you have a choice of possible strategies or ways of responding. The trouble with most people is that they forget this fact and become enamored of one particular response. After a while their response is so predictable that potential attackers can turn them into victims almost without effort. Take a moment to see if you can identify the way in which you usually respond to attack. Do you yell? Scream? Cry? Run? Try to remember the last conflict you were engaged in and describe how you dealt with it. If you can't remember exactly how you behaved, then try putting yourself in the following situation.

THE PARKING SPACE

It's two o'clock in the morning in a large, crowded city. You're alone in your car. Parking spaces are at a premium. There's one space vacant immediately outside the place you are staying for the night and there's an all-night parking garage twenty blocks away. The near space is free; the garage will cost you five dollars for the night.

You and another driver reach the space at the same time. Neither car can have the space unless the other car moves. What do you do?

Be as honest with yourself as you can and note down on a piece of paper what you think your actual response would be. (And remember, it's two o'clock in the morning.) Would you:

1) argue with the other driver?
2) wait him out?
3) forget about the space and drive to the parking garage?
4) call a cop?
5) try reasoning with the other driver?
6) do something else?

Now let's try the same situation again, adding some other components. How do you respond if:

1) the other driver is bigger than you?
2) the other driver is smaller than you?
3) you have a very important job interview early the next morning?
4) the other driver tells you he has a sick wife upstairs and needs to get back to her quickly, but you are not sure whether he is lying?

5) you have a passenger with you in the car, with whom you are madly in love?

Write down what you feel your real-life responses would be in each of those situations, given the circumstances we've indicated.

Are all your responses of one particular type? In other words, are you more likely to argue than you are to say "the hell with it" and drive to the all-night garage? Or are you more likely to try to reason with the other driver? See if you can find a pattern to your responses.

Now you should have a pretty good idea of what type of conflictor you are: a fighter, an avoider, a talker, a white-liar, a cop-caller, or whatever. There's nothing inherently wrong with any of these responses to conflict. What is wrong is your tendency to handle all your conflicts in exactly the same way. A balanced approach to conflict management calls for a carefully considered response which is appropriate to each event. Attack-tics will teach you that there are many options open to you when you need to respond.

Now let's look at a classic head-to-head confrontation to find out just what those options are. The confrontation is between Robin Hood and Little John. They might as well be in two cars as on foot, and the footbridge might as well be the one remaining parking space.

THE ROBIN HOOD GAME*

Presently [Robin] came to a place where a brook ran across the road. Horses went through a ford, but foot passengers could cross by a long narrow, wooden bridge, without a hand-

*From *Robin Hood*, published by the John C. Winston Company, 1923.

rail. Robin stepped on the bridge to walk across, and at the very instant that he did so, a huge fellow, a very giant of a man, stepped on the farther end. Each moved forward briskly, thinking that the other would give way, and they met in the middle of the bridge.

. . . Robin made test of him at once.

"Give way, my man!" he cried. "What meant ye by stepping on the bridge when you saw that I was about to come over, and that the bridge is not wide enough for two?"

The stranger carried, besides his sword, a huge quarterstaff, full seven feet long, thick and heavy, a tremendous cudgel. He now quietly leaned upon it and smiled as he said, "And why should I stand aside for you, archer? Let me tell you that I have never stood aside for any man yet, and see no reason to begin this day."

So Robin laid aside his great bow of Spanish yew and his quiver of sharp-pointed arrows, and ran to a thicket beside the stream, and cut himself a stout staff of ground oak. When he came back with his stick the stranger was still resting on his quarterstaff in the middle of the bridge.

"Here will we fight where we have met," cried Robin Hood, "and the man who knocks the other into the stream shall be the winner."

"Agreed!" cried the gigantic stranger, and the two combatants faced each other warily, setting their feet cautiously on the narrow planking, and grasping their staves about midway of the length in order to be ready for assault or defense.

For a few moments the two champions whirled their sticks about, feinting, striking, parrying, each searching for an opening in the other's guard. Robin was the first to get in a body blow. He pretended to strike at the stranger's head; the latter raised his staff swiftly to parry, and Robin, changing his hold and the direction of his blow with wonderful speed and dexterity, caught his opponent a tremendous thwack across the ribs.

The giant gave a growl of anger, and replied with such a

terrific slashing cut that no man could have stood before it. But Robin dodged it nimbly, and replied with a smart rap across the shoulder. But even as this fell the stranger whirled his staff in his hands, and launched a shrewd stroke at Robin's head. Nothing but Robin's quickness saved him from being knocked headlong into the stream, and as it was he did not altogether escape. The big man's staff glanced across his head, cut his crown, and caused the blood to stream down the side of his face.

This put Robin in such a rage that he dealt a whole shower of blows at his opponent with such swiftness that the tall man was kept entirely on the defensive. He was forced to parry, parry, parry all the time.

Time and again Robin's quick staff got home on the big man's body, but the tall fellow never gave way an inch, but fought stoutly on. Suddenly the giant repaid Robin Hood's many thwacks once and for all. Gathering all his tremendous strength, he brought down his great staff with all the power of his long arms and mighty body. Robin parried, but though his stick was held correctly, he might as well have tried to parry a thunderbolt. Down came the crashing blow. It broke Robin Hood's staff in two, it fell with but little diminished force on Robin's body, and hurled him flying into the brook.

"Ha, ha, Master Archer!" laughed the stranger merrily; "Where art thou now?"

"By my faith . . . me thinks I am in the brook fairly enough, and thou hast won the bout. But I'll freely say thou hast won fairly."

We'll warrant it has been no mean number of years since most of you have read that section, and certainly the behavior and the writing style seem far removed from our modern age. It's always a shock to see that Robin scurries off the bridge to get a staff and that Little John actually waits for him to come back instead of taking advantage of the absence to complete his trip! But, as romantic as it is, is it so far removed from everyday life? Every day you see Robin Hood and Little John on a crowded sidewalk. They carry attaché cases instead of quarterstaffs, but they're just as bound and determined not to give way. Businessmen play arbitration scenes just as full of contradictions and impasses as Robin Hood's. And there are days in most marriages when the wife is on one end of the narrow bridge and the husband on the other and the kids surely know that somebody's going to end up in the water! It seems to us that this story is an excellent metaphor for most conflicts we face.

It's obvious that Robin and Little John made a conscious decision to fight, thus making the event into a contest—a classic win/lose situation. What other strategies were open to them?

For one thing, either Robin or Little John could have run away. So *withdrawal* is another option that was open.

For another, they could have *parleyed:* discussed the problem, assessed their priorities, and reached some kind of compromise. Robin could have told Little John that he needed to get across the bridge first because of some pressing business with the Sheriff of Nottingham, and Little John could have given way, admitting that he was just out for a stroll.

For yet another, each could have decided to *do nothing.* They could have waited each other out, standing quietly, to see what would happen.

Still another option they could have employed is *deception.* Little John could have yelled, "Bear! Run like hell!"

And, finally, unique to Attack-tics is the sixth conflict option, Aiki (pronounced "éye-key"), meaning in Japanese "confluence." We'll see in detail how this works later on.

To recap, then, in any conflict situation we have the following options open to us:

1) Fighting Back
2) Withdrawal

3) Parley
4) Doing Nothing
5) Deception
6) Aiki (Confluence)

It is of paramount importance to understand that in At-tack-tics these options do not contain within them any value connotations whatsoever. So long as they are *consciously* applied, they are neither good nor bad, neither right nor wrong. They are appropriate to an event of conflict or they are inappropriate to an event of conflict. Therefore, as you proceed through this book try to forget all your previous notions that "fight" is good and manly and "Doing Nothing" is bad and cowardly. Dismiss as soon as possible your idea that Withdrawal is escapism or poor sportsmanship. Parley is neither more reasonable nor unreasonable than any of the other modes of response. Doing Nothing is not copping out; it is doing nothing. Deception is not a sin, it is a means of handling an attacker. It's not more fun or less worthy than any of the other options.

The sooner you can discard the usual connotations of these words, the sooner you will become more proficient at handling attack. Experience shows that wading through word-affects will only slow you down.

Because it is attack we're talking about here, and your response to attack. But our system is not designed to show you how to attack someone else. It is not designed to show you more ways to do somebody in. The focus of Attack-tics is on helping you deal with people who step on you, people who make unprovoked (so far as you're concerned) attacks on your person, your personality, your emotions, and your sense of yourself as a human being.

We shall presume throughout what follows that you are the *recipient* of an attack, *not* the instigator of a conflict. The six options—Fighting Back, Withdrawal, Parley,

Doing Nothing, Deception, and Aiki (Confluence)—are your options only when you are the target of someone else's aggression.

So now let's examine your conflict options one by one, with some hints on how and when each is best employed. And why.

IV

Your Conflict Options

1. FIGHTING BACK

In the Attack-tics system, the attacker is symbolized by the upper, shaded, triangle:

If two people are engaged in attack and Fighting Back, the event is represented like this:

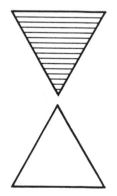

Throughout the book the person who is attacked, the You figure, will be represented by the *lower* geometric shape. Later, in the chapter on geometry, you will see exactly how these symbols interact. In the meantime, it is worth noting here that the choice of the triangle—pointed toward the conflict—is not capricious. The shape, the geometry of the triangle, carries with it the essence of the focused attack: *the thrust forward from a strong base.* The angularity of the form even suggests the clash of wills, principles, or forces. (As we shall see with the other responses, other geometric forms denote wholly different feelings.)

Even as we write, we're conscious of the fact that Fighting Back is one of the most counterproductive responses in most conflict situations. Certainly it is the least wisely and most widely used tactic in the whole lexicon of conflict.

ATTACKER: You're a dummy!
YOU: You're an idiot!
ATTACKER: You stink!
YOU: Your mother wears army boots!

If this doesn't bring back memories of the neighborhood playground, nothing will. Those were (and, sadly, continue to be) the kind of responses which failed us most often:

MOTHER: When are you going to get married?
DAUGHTER: It's none of your business!
MOTHER: How can you talk to me this way!
DAUGHTER: Why are you always on my back!
MOTHER: You're ungrateful!
DAUGHTER: You're hateful!

There really isn't much distance between this argument and the one in the playground scene. Nobody ever "wins" these fights, and no kind of resolution or harmony—and that remains our goal—ever comes out of them.

And yet there *are* times when Fighting Back is the most appropriate response to a conflict situation.

WHEN TO FIGHT BACK

Fighting Back should be your last alternative after you have decided there is no Withdrawing, no chance for Parley, for Deception, or for Confluence, and you must do something. In other words, Fighting Back is your last resort.

And we're quite serious about that. You have to learn to resist that first impulse to lash out wildly at your attacker. There are many cases where people have fought a mugger and lost their lives. Had they chosen another response, they might have lived.

Fight Back when it is a question of life or death (yours or someone else's) and you have no other options open to you.

The decision is yours, and you must weigh it as objectively as you can to make sure you have indeed run out of other options. However, when it's a question of survival, life gives you the right to Fight Back.

Fighting Back can be the most appropriate response to conflict when it is a question of serious priority which directly affects your life.

Just what constitutes *serious priority?* Again, you must be the judge of that. But bear in mind that ego—your desire not to look bad—often disguises itself as *serious priority.* Let's say you're sure you're fighting for something really major. In the heat of the argument you hear yourself shouting: "Ah, but it's the principle of the thing!" That should be a tipoff to you. If you're engaged in a conflict and you hear yourself saying "It's the principle of the thing," stop Fighting Back and examine other options, other strategies. Sometimes you *will* be fighting for a principle of serious priority; if that's the case, though, you won't need to remind yourself or your opponent of that fact. You don't fight religious persecution or racial prejudice and cry "I'm only fighting for the principle of equality!" You just fight. And yet we're constantly faced with people who Fight Back about the fair distribution of labor when they just want to get out of doing the laundry!

Remember, it's okay to Fight Back for a principle, but only if the principle is of serious priority.

Actually, all we ask is that you raise to consciousness the reasons by which you make your choice of options. Make your decisions with all the objectivity of which you are capable.

To review, Fighting Back is the appropriate response when 1) all other options are closed or exhausted; 2) it is a question of life or death; or 3) it is a question of serious priority. Obviously, especially when you're in physical jeopardy, it's not always possible to stand by idly, checking your options and turning every event into a cognitive jigsaw puzzle ("Wait a minute, boss, I'm trying to figure out if I should Withdraw or beat the crap outa you . . ."). So many of our daily conflicts come up so fast that we have to trust our intuition, our gut reactions. But those reactions should be *informed* reactions, and Attack-tics is a way of tuning them up, of bringing to consciousness the possibilities that might have eluded you before.

BEFORE YOU FIGHT BACK

Now that you have the "whens" of Fighting Back pretty
well in hand, there are two elements of this conflict option
you need to consider before launching any good defensive
reaction: overall rules and estimates of the situation.

Rules of Fighting Back

Rule #1: You must know at as deep a level as possible that
*you have the right to life, and the entire universe sanctions
your right to fight to preserve it.* When you know this rule
well, you can enter into any struggle with total commitment.
Your adversary will sense your spirit, and if he has any sense,
he'll withdraw.

Rule #2. The corollary to Rule #1 is: *Never Fight Back
against anyone who has nothing to lose.* Find another way
out. Suppose, for example, you surprise an intruder in your
home and he's sufficiently off balance or cornered or psy-
chopathic to be ready to toss his life away rather than be
apprehended. *Get out of the way.* Likewise, if you're up
against a person who doesn't care whether you fire him or
not, a person who's completely ready to put his whole being
on the line, be aware of it and don't let your sense of heroics
force you into Fighting Back.

Rule #3. The third basic rule of Fighting Back, and one
of the most important to internalize, is: *Use the minimum
force necessary to restore harmony.* Your emotions may sig-
nal you to go for the throat, to kill, maim, or traumatize, but
your heart must speak louder. Your job is to restore harmony, not to punish. Your focus should be on solving the
problem, not on ruining some poor slob's self-image. Too
often the teenager who spends two hours in the shower in the

morning is attacked by his parents with the amount of force the FBI might use on a highjacker.

Rule #4. The extension of Rule #3 is that *you must never extend your counterattack beyond the possibility of return.* To give too much is as damaging as to give too little. Too much force is not only a sign that you're unbalanced; it's unwise, because you will have overreacted to the point where you can be easily destroyed. You're raging and ranting so much that your attacker need only shrug his shoulders and suggest you go somewhere for extended psychotherapy. You realize you've turned purple and made a fool of yourself.

Rule #5. *Don't Fight Back if you don't have to.*

Estimating the Situation

No one expects you to Fight Back blindly, without having first assessed all the variables of each conflict situation. You can say, "Hey, I can't go through all this and estimate when I'm being yelled at by my husband!" but we're going to suggest that if you *don't* go through all this and estimate the situation, you're going to be defeated—or else the defeat of your opponent will be irreversible.

A good pre-fight estimate should include the following kinds of concerns:

1) relationship
2) place
3) time
4) spirit

Relationship: What is the relationship between you and the person attacking you? It seems like an obvious point, but why then are most homicides between friends? If either participant in the struggle stopped and realized that he was fighting a friend or lover (and acknowledged all that that entails) the statistics on homicide would change radically. It would, at least, defuse the unthinking passion of the moment.

Place: Take half a millisecond to ask yourself if this is the best place to engage in a fight. Do you really want to yell and be yelled at in the elevator? in the hallway, in front of a dozen witnesses? in the bedroom? If it isn't the right place, if you are at a distinct disadvantage, don't stand there like a turkey on the day before Thanksgiving—move! You can try any number of strategies. The best is the most direct: "If you want to have an argument, let's go where we can do it fairly." You can then move to your office, the broom closet, the living room, the park, or wherever is best for you. There is no reason on earth why you must Fight Back on somebody else's turf.

Time: Is this really the best time to Fight Back? It's possible you may not be able to control this element, but you shouldn't have to be at anybody else's mercy, either. You have the right to say, "Look, I'm tired right now, and you're asking me to deal with a very difficult problem. I can't help you solve it at this moment." If you keep getting caught on somebody else's clock, you'll be stuck every time. Not every conflict has to be dealt with at the time of the infraction. You do have some power. Use it.

The other aspect of time is timing. You have to sense when the right moment for the right fact and right statement comes along. It won't do to have you shoot your whole force on the opening salvo. You're an intelligent person, and you can do a whole lot better in your fights by being more sensitive to timing than to your bruised ego.

Spirit: Finally, and just as important as all the preceding, is the recognition of spirit—yours and your opponent's. When you fight, you should focus on a clean, clear intention informed by a protective spirit. You know exactly what you want, and you are there to protect every living thing involved in the conflict: you, your opponent, and everyone else who'll be affected by the outcome of the fight. To fight in any other way is contrary to the spirit of Attack-tics, contrary to the life principle, and ultimately self-defeating, since *every vanquished foe is a potential adversary.* If that doesn't frighten you, you might as well exchange this book for a Smith and Wesson .38-caliber revolver and a box of ammunition. Remember, no matter how paradoxical it may seem, Fighting Back is used to help your attacker restore his or her balance —not to pump up your ego. If you can adopt that kind of protective spirit, you'll begin to experience life in a completely new way.

HOW TO FIGHT BACK

Now that we've covered the basics of when to Fight Back and all the rules and estimates of the fight, let's see how Attack-tics uses Fighting Back as a conflict option.

Fighting Back is probably one of the most difficult responses to carry out well. Very few of us have been taught how. What we've learned—and a great deal of it is wrong— we've picked up through hard, sometimes tragic, experience. Often our usual response is based upon the past—in other words, what we've gotten away with before. If screaming at the school bully works when we are ten years old, we tend to become screamers. If idle threats (convincingly delivered) destroy an older sibling, then in adulthood we will probably run around threatening everybody who'll listen to us. And so it goes.

As we go around in our workshops, eavesdropping on people who have just begun to Fight Back, we find that the average man or woman employing this response to conflict loses control, loses his or her balance. Because control is gone, he makes, among others, the following kinds of mistakes: He employs too much force; he makes bad estimates of the situation; he fights unfairly; or he goes too far to restore harmony and can only destroy.

"Emotional" is the operative word. There's no completely "cool" way to enter into a conflict, but we have to learn to be a lot less hysterical than we usually are. (The next chapter, on centering, will go a long way toward solving this problem.) But here we are, with the adrenalin soaring through our bodies, our balance gone, voices from the past screaming at us, and we feel, above all else, fear.

And so we overreact . . . usually. And molehills become veritable Everests. The only resolution that most of us aim for is silence: the silence of a completely vanquished foe; the silence of an enemy who quietly plots another attack.

It doesn't have to be that way; it *must* not be that way.

To Fight Back well, you must look at "the fight" in three stages: immobilization, control, and the restoration of harmony.

Stage #1: Immobilization

"Immobilization" means pretty much what it says. Before you can solve a conflict with a serious opponent, you must stop his or her advance so that you can exert control over the situation. How you do this is up to you. You can use a stern expression, take a step inside your opponent's space, say "Now, you hold on! I will not be insulted!" Use your ingenuity to stop your opponent's onslaught in the first stage of the fight.

Stage #2: Control

You've stopped the attacker's advance. Control is more difficult to establish. Control is the result of the force of your argument; you are, in effect, leading your opponent to see things from your perspective, to understand where he's made his error, to refrain from keeping the fight going out of spite or arrogance. You stand the best chance for succeeding at control by fighting fair and staying specific.

Unfair fighting in human relationships only causes your opponent to fight harder, to become more unbalanced. Examples of unfair fighting, "hitting below the belt," include the use of sarcasm, making personal remarks, and fighting the person rather than trying to solve the problem: "What idiot spilled the coffee on the rug?" It seems to us that the problem is the coffee stain, not the "idiot."

Remember, no matter what kind of fighting your opponent gets into, retain your balance. Then all his insults won't help him, no matter what he thinks. If you get tripped up and begin name-calling, you'll be in as precarious a position as he is. Your job is not to anger your opponent, but to seek harmony.

Generalizations and exaggerations make it difficult for you to control an opponent. *Stay specific.* The temptation in any argument is to validate your stand by saying things like "Everybody in the *world* knows you can't use a butter knife for a screwdriver!" "You always, *always* say 'yes' when you mean 'no'!" In any relationship of some duration there is the tendency to explode a two-day habit into a lifetime lack of discipline: *"For the past six years* you've done nothing but mope around the house all day!" Actually, it's only been a two-hour depression.

Even though you're fighting hand to hand and head to head, you must stay on balance and quote specific instances, being as accurate as you can. It doesn't matter one whit that your opponent is tossing up sarcasm, insults, made-up statistics. Your job is to keep advancing with clear intention and all deliberate speed to regain control of the situation. For example:

MACK: What idiot spilled the coffee on the rug!

YOU: Let's get a rag and some cold water.

MACK: How clumsy can you get!

YOU: I didn't spill it, but while you're screaming the coffee's staining the rug. Grab a sponge.

Certainly not an earth-leveling argument, but it points out rather simply how important it is to stay on point, on balance, keeping your triangle aimed straight at the problem even though your opponent is all over the place. It works just as well when the fight is more serious:

MACK: If I ever get the chance, I'm going to see you canned!

YOU: I won't let you get the chance. What's the problem?

MACK: You're a jerk!

YOU: You want to solve the problem or get your anger out at me?

In each instance the You character kept his triangle on target, aimed at the conflict and working for control.

Stage #3: The Restoration of Harmony

Though a stage in itself, *the restoration of harmony is the goal of all conflict.* Keeping that in mind will restrain you from making "killer statements"—attacks which wound an opponent so much that harmony can never be restored. You can't tell somebody he was never good in bed and then expect things to go back to the way they used to be between you. The wound will remain (especially if it's true).

Instead of standing with one foot on the carcass of your opponent—as we've been taught to do by our society—you must work very hard to find a way in which both combatants "win," a way in which both feel good about themselves. *The best "victory" is the one in which everyone wins.* The way to achieve that combined "win" is to focus on the problem at all points along the way. Once control is established, you will ideally have both combatants side by side, working together on a mutually agreeable solution. That is what harmony is about. Just as with the spilled coffee, the two of you are down on your hands and knees, taking care of the spill.

PHYSICAL ATTITUDE

What about the very important area of nonverbal communication? While we have been focusing on words up to this point—what kinds of things to say and not to say—it is equally important that when you choose to Fight Back you say the right things *without* words. Bodies, faces, and physical relationships can say as much as two hundred paragraphs' worth of well-chosen, harmonious words.

For example, let's say you're doing very well with the verbiage, attacking the problem and so forth, but your eyes are narrow slits, your hands are on your hips, your left foot is advanced, and you're two inches away from your opponent's face. That may be the appropriate physical attitude if you're coming down heavily on someone, but it just doesn't go with those new words you're saying—words that are meant to restore harmony. You may be reciting poetry, but if your whole demeanor is attacking the person, he'll feel it.

Know what your body is saying.

There are three elements of physical attitude to keep in mind: face, posture, and spatial relationship. Let's look at them one by one.

Your face can be the most expressive part of your body. That's terrific except for the fact that it can and does express things you're not even aware of. You must begin to look in the mirror for things other than blemishes. You've got to know what your expressions look like—and what they feel like. Stand at the mirror and ask your face to look angry. Observe how that feels in all the muscles of your face. Memorize the sensations. Then go on and do the same with "sad," "confused," "afraid," and "happy." As you deal with people in and out of conflict, monitor your face. Know that you're off kilter when you say you're happy but your face *feels* sad. Get back on the right track.

We constantly observe in our work people who are Fighting Back but giving away their "true" fears. They come on very heavy, but their eyes are wide and their mouths are slackly open. Or they try to Fight Back but their eyes appear to be crying. Their opponents may not be careful observers themselves, but people do sense this disequilibrium.

The "right" face for Fighting Back is probably the blankest face. It looks its opponent square between the eyes (so as not to become caught off guard by looking *into* the eyes) and lets the protective spirit keep the expression as neutral—but powerful—as possible. An angry or hostile face tends to challenge the opponent, making the resolution of conflict all the more difficult.

Posture must also become raised to the conscious level. Watch people engaged in conflict. Observe how bodies express their owners' emotions. The word "overbearing" aptly describes the taller person who leans over and down on his victim. Parents are often unaware of how their hands-on-hips ("I'm fed up with you!") stance frightens their children. People who make their points with their index fingers are rarely aware of the threat contained in that gesture.

As with the face, the point is to know what your body says and make sure it's saying what you want it to. Don't Fight Back verbally while you are leaning backward. Don't poke someone in the sternum and say, "Look, I only want to deal with the problem!" Stand comfortably.

Keep your posture consistent with your approach.

Finally, what is your spatial relationship to your opponent? Few of us are aware of the concept of our personal space. We live in our space, walk in it, sit in it, and converse in it, but we're rarely conscious of it until someone comes into it uninvited. Think of what it feels like to talk to somebody who talks right into your face. What if you keep backing up and he keeps coming forward?

Observe your space and begin to sense the space of others —especially when you are engaged in conflict. There are times, as when you are being severe, when you must march right into somebody else's space and demand that he or she cease and desist from some kind of behavior. There are other times when that kind of invasion would be the worst thing —as when you're dealing with a child and you're looking for a mutually acceptable solution.

Know how to use your space to maximize your chances for harmony.

SUMMING UP

To aid you in Fighting Back we've included a checklist. Refer to it and memorize it.

When to Fight Back
   1) There is no other option.
   2) It is a question of life or death.
   3) It is a question of serious priority.

Rules of Fighting
   1) You have the right to life, and the entire universe sanctions your right to fight to preserve it.
   2) Never fight anyone who has nothing to lose.
   3) Use the minimum force necessary to restore harmony.
   4) Never extend your counterattack beyond the possibility of return.

5) Don't fight if you don't have to.

Estimating the Situation

1) *Relationship:* What is the relationship between me and my attacker?

2) *Place:* Is this the best place to fight?

3) *Time:* Is this the best time to fight? What is the proper timing of my counterattack?

4) *Spirit:* How committed is my attacker? How committed am I?

Three Stages of Fighting Back

1) *Immobilization:* to stop an attacker's advance.

2) *Control:* to focus the conflict on the problem by fighting fair and staying specific.

3) *Restoration of Harmony:* the "victory" in which both sides "win" and the real problem is resolved.

Physical Attitude

1) *Face:* What is it saying? What do I want it to say?

2) *Posture:* What is it saying? What do I want it to say? What are my hands saying? What should they say?

3) *Spatial relationship:* Where am I in relationship to my opponent's space?

At first it will seem an impossible job—this estimating and thinking and checking and questioning. If you try, though, you will find that it soon becomes a substitute for your less successful past attempts to Fight Back. The rewards are immediate, and that alone should encourage you to continue. If you fail and get "tricked" back into your old modes of behavior, the world will not come to an end. Just get back on the track and try again.

You can do it.

2. WITHDRAWAL

If fighting has a bad press in our culture, nothing could be worse, we are told, than running away.

We'd like to change that image.

In order to use this response, first you must rid yourself of all the intimations of cowardice that are attached to "running away." If you Fight Back, rather than flee, because you think flight is cowardly, then you've made a bad mistake. If you fight rather than flee because you didn't know you could flee, you are making the same error.

In the Attack-tics system, Withdrawal is represented by the triangle pointed away from the point of conflict:

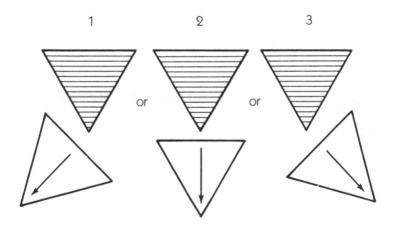

The point of the triangle is directed cleanly in another direction; it is not a scattered retreat, not confused, not apologetic. Too often people, unless being chased by a bear or a raving lunatic, run in circles, as if their clothes were on fire, jump up and down like Keystone Kops, or fall apart and offer themselves up for destruction. The triangle is a reminder that Withdrawal is the specific choice, that it is a strategy that must be employed with the same balance and calm used in any other strategy. *It is directed.*

WHEN TO WITHDRAW

Withdrawal is an appropriate response in the following kinds of situations:

When all else fails and an escape route is open to you. In the physical sense, this response is obvious. You are Fighting Back against a bruiser and losing. If you spend much longer at it, you'll be broken in two. Unless you're a romantic with decidedly masochistic tendencies, there's little glory to be had in hanging around for Armageddon. You run as fast as you can if you still can . . ."to fight another day." In the realm of verbal conflict, Withdrawal is tougher to visualize, because it doesn't always involve leaving the scene.

Sadly, where Withdrawal is not employed often enough is in male-female relationships. When all the conflicts have become fights and every attempt at resolution has failed, then Withdrawal can be far superior to patiently enduring the constant warfare. In our workshops we are forever meeting men and women who tell us of marriages marked by physical and emotional brutality. When we ask the individuals why they don't leave, they say: "I'm trying to save the marriage" or "I'm staying in it for the sake of the children" or "It may work out by itself." In these cases it would probably take a lot more inner strength to Withdraw than to stay and do battle. There are hundreds of studies to show that children are just as harmed by waiting out a bad relationship as by divorce. Moreover, we are increasingly convinced that when someone has to "work" to save a marriage, the marriage or the individuals in it are inevitably going to suffer.

Thus, Withdrawal of a temporary or permanent nature should be considered by people who find themselves in bad marriages, bad relationships, conflict-ridden jobs, etc. We must begin to stop thinking of life as something that must be borne as if we were Spartans and the world our battleground. With this provision—that all other avenues have been found less effective or unworkable.

When time and place are wrong. As we discovered in the section on Fighting Back, the time and place must be right or the conflict will turn into defeat. Therefore, when you choose to Withdraw do so as soon as possible; as they said in the old war movies, "Let's get the hell out of here!"

For example, Noreen is a salesclerk in a small boutique. From time to time she must deal with customers who are, to say the least, abrasive. Some are just rude, but others, like Mrs. Bradford, are downright abusive. Mrs. Bradford is a member of that large society whose members make themselves feel better by tormenting people in "lesser stations" in life. It's irrelevant why this group acts the way it does—our job is to survive them, to keep from feeling bad about ourselves because of their win/lose philosophy of life. We shall see later that Noreen has other options open to her, but on this occasion Withdrawal is what she comes up with. She's decided that the time and place are wrong.

The store is crowded. It's just before Christmas, and the shoppers have caught one another's hysteria. Noreen and the temporary help are overworked and tired. It's a half-hour before closing time.

Mrs. Bradford collars Noreen and instantly begins ranting

about the incorrect size label on a dress she bought the week before. At first Noreen manages well. She apologizes on behalf of the store and agrees to make good on the error as simply as possible. But that is not enough for Mrs. Bradford, whose subconscious is rejoicing at the opportunity to rage against the world and all its inhabitants. She is not satisfied with the offer. She raises her voice:

> MRS. BRADFORD: This is typical of this store! It's apparent that you people go out of your way to inconvenience your customers!

As Noreen looks around she sees that many of her customers are tuning in to the conflict; the store's reputation is in jeopardy. She also knows that Mrs. Bradford is not to be put off with apologies or excuses, that Fighting Back will only result in a holocaust. The place is wrong—not in a crowded store where "the customer is always right"—and the time is wrong—just before closing.

Noreen decides to Withdraw.

But where can she run to? It would hardly be appropriate for her to wheel around and run out of the store—and out on her job.

Withdrawal is not necessarily physical.

Noreen centers herself (more on this later), remains calm, and responds as unemotionally as possible.

> NOREEN: Mrs. Bradford, I'm not the person for you to talk to about this. I'm only a clerk here. If you wish to speak to the manager, please leave me your telephone number and I'll have her call you as soon as she gets in. Excuse me now, I must wait on these people. They've been waiting a long time and I don't want to disappoint them. Thanks for your patience.

With that she smiles and turns very effectively to do the job she's paid for.

Of course, it's possible that Mrs. Bradford will continue to rant and rave, but if the Withdrawal is triangular, made deliberately and confidently, the angry woman will be thrown off balance. The "thanks," a gift from Noreen, should help her regain her sense of humanity. The other customers, hearing Noreen's statement about not disappointing them, are now won over to her side. Most importantly, she has made a clean break with the action and removed herself from a conflict that might have resulted in her losing more than her temper.

Ah, you say, but what about how Noreen feels inside? How can she let an old harridan get away with such behavior?

Noreen isn't letting Mrs. Bradford get away with anything. Mrs. Bradford is Mrs. Bradford, and Noreen is Noreen. Even though at this moment they occupy the same space-and-time droplet, it isn't up to Noreen to pay the woman back by defeating her. Noreen's self-image, and a positive one at that, comes from her ability to handle conflict, not from being able to wallop an angry old woman.

Now let's see how Withdrawal is employed in another conflict situation. Bob is a divorced man who meets Ken, an old friend, at a cocktail party. After too many drinks, Ken turns to Bob and says: "Bob, I hear you only hang out with married women. You scared of *real* women? I never thought of you as a coward!"

Bob could Fight Back. But what would be the point? This is hardly a case of life-or-death or serious priority. Although a number of other options are open, Bob, deciding that this is hardly the time or place to discuss his private life, chooses Withdrawal. Turning to face Ken squarely, he says, "Excuse me, Ken, but I don't wish to speak about it." And off he goes across the floor to talk to anybody he chooses. He's flown from the conflict which Ken set up for him. Knowing there can be no winner in this situation, he excuses himself and moves away—Withdraws. To our way of thinking, only somebody who is desperately looking for attention any way he can find it would hang around and get embroiled in armchair psychiatry with a drunken friend who feels abusive. There's nothing there to be won.

Again, self-esteem comes from handling yourself well and being pleased with yourself, not from becoming entangled in conflict and wiping out somebody else. It doesn't matter a bit whether Ken is correct; Bob has the right to Withdraw.

HOW TO WITHDRAW

The hows of leaving a conflict couldn't be simpler. You must Withdraw clearly and with a single intention.

Too often we find people who give off two signals. In other words, they Withdraw but they do it ambiguously, giving the other person the feeling that they really want to be asked to stay. They are unclear about their right to leave the scene, and so their Withdrawal is wishy-washy. For example, a person who, when leaving, says "I'll be back" or "Don't think you're getting away with anything" or "My return will depend on how you behave" is really trying to fight and run at the same time. All that does is confuse the opponent.

So, if you've chosen to Withdraw, make sure you do it with certainty, knowing that you are exercising your right to stay out of destructive involvements. (Later, when you learn to center yourself, you'll understand better how to make a centered Withdrawal and avoid ambiguous moves.)

One last time: You must separate all valuations from the concept of Withdrawal in order to use it well. If you hesitate for an instant because of some holdover about cowardice or loss of face, you are lost.

3. PARLEY

In the Attack-tics system, Parley is represented by a triangle (the aggressor) faced by a circle (your response):

For the first time in this chapter we can deal straightforwardly without having to seem to apologize for a strategy. Parley—the reasoned exchange of possible solutions, the discussion of possible outcomes—is looked on with favor in our culture. The art of compromise and arbitration is held in high esteem. Former Secretary of State Kissinger used to Parley on the international front, while skilled arbiters like Theodore Kheel are renowned for their efforts on the national scene. Police officers are regularly taught that the longer a felon or even a potential suicide is kept talking, the greater the chance for mutual survival. There are many good books in the professional libraries covering strategies and tactics for compromise.

But Parley is not always the best choice of conflict options. One doesn't, for example, find it easy to compromise one's ideals and principles. And there is rarely a half-decent chance to compromise in life-and-death situations. We'd be hard put to share a solution with a mugger if we played by his rules:

"Just hit me on my right side and take only half my money and we'll get along fine . . ."

So, too, in the world of social conflict, there are situations where Parley would be the inappropriate choice of conflict response.

"You're right to question my Catholic faith. I tell you what—if you leave me alone, I promise to believe in only one third of the Trinity!"

Hardly. You deserve better than that. You have a right to your beliefs, your principles, your ethics.

Parley is represented by the circle to denote the fact that the responder is neither Fighting Back nor Withdrawing. In truth, one who chooses to Parley is doing a bit of both: not giving up everything, and doing some turning around. So, even though Parley is essentially an act of circularity, of turning and giving in to a degree, it is *not* passive. Parley is a means or strategy of compromising to reach a solution.

Okay, so there are times when Parley is the best, meaning "most appropriate," response to an event of conflict. Robin Hood is coming charging across that log and there you are. You can discuss things "like rational human beings." But which log, at what time, is best for compromise? Which situation? Which adversary?

WHEN TO PARLEY

Parley is most effective when you are involved in a no-win situation. Your adversary may have defined the event as a contest with a winner and a loser, but it's often up to you— because you're a together, centered human being—to turn (circularize) the conflict around and offer a reasonable way out for both parties. You decide that there doesn't need to be a winner or a loser, and you point the way toward maximizing both your own and your opponent's gains.

Abby is your six-year-old daughter. She paddles downstairs in her Dr. Dentons and attacks, her cute little smile turned into a pout:

> ABBY: Louise's parents let her stay up later'n me. *She's* got really *nice* parents.

Instantly your sensors go on red alert: *This is a no-win situation.* Of course, you could Fight Back, arguing that Louise's parents are usually so stoned they don't know where their daughter is, and in fact you are really better parents than they are. We doubt, however, that Abby would appreciate or understand this information. Moreover, there are no known "perfect" tests for good parenting anyway. One set of parents would say that a good parent hits when necessary; another would say that a good parent never hits. You know kids from strict homes and kids from "lax" homes who are nice or rotten or whatever, so there is *no way to win* on this issue by Fighting Back.

You could Withdraw from little Abby, telling her you have to go to the bathroom, but the attack hardly warrants that, and anyway, Abby is a persistent kid. You might throw her off balance for a while, but she'd still come back to the subject of staying up for an extra half-hour.

The important thing however, is that you've sensed it's a no-win situation. Not that there couldn't be a winner—you *could* simply tie her to the closet door and turn off all the lights. You, the strong one, would in effect be the winner, and Abby, the weakling, would be the loser. In name, anyway; reason tells us that both Abby and her parents are losers when events are viewed that way. Then if the parents have a soul, they end up feeling guilty, and Abby winds up running away from home.

So you, the parent, sit down to work it out, compromise, Parley with Abby about her problem.

HOW TO PARLEY

Rule #1: Parley requires two circles after the initial stage.

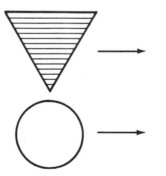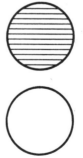

Figure 1. Initial Stage   Figure 2. Parley

In other words, after you've told your adversary that you are willing to work out a compromise, talk it over, look at it from both sides, you need to have *two* compromisers. Parley is not the art of giving up everything; it is the art of making mutually acceptable deals, finding a harmonious resolution.

On your part, this may mean being a little less rigid about bedtime. You might agree, on Abby's terms, to ask around and see what other parents feel is a reasonable bedtime. (This will require your being freer with your ego, being willing to concede "error" in some measure, and being prepared to treat Abby as having equal rights. But that act on your part will go a long way toward making Abby a reasonable human being too . . .) Or you might offer a deal: make her bedtime tie in directly with the condition of her room. Remember, however, you are not tricking her into or out of anything. You are two equal people engaged in the solution of a problem.

It isn't easy.

First you will have to determine just what is underneath Abby's complaint about good parenting and bedtime. The art of compromise does not mean you must of necessity stick to the first issue brought up. In dealing with children (and with big people, too) sometimes you have to help them look beneath their stated desires to watch an extra fifteen minutes of *Starsky and Hutch*. It is altogether possible that Abby just wants a little attention. If you Fight Back and yell her down, she'll have gotten the attention, negative though it be, and nothing much will have been solved. You'll end up furious, frustrated, guilty, and thinking ill of yourself. It is much more difficult, at times, to Parley. Yet see how effective that option can be:

ABBY: Louise's parents let her stay up later'n me. *She's* got really *nice* parents.

    YOU: What is it you'd like to do?
    ABBY: Watch *Starsky and Hutch*. Louise's parents always let
          her watch it.
    YOU: I guess we've really been busy lately, haven't we? We
          haven't given you all the attention you'd like to have.
    ABBY: I don't know . . .
    YOU: What time does Louise have to go to bed?
    ABBY: I don't know . . .

At this point you have the choice of being exasperated
with her nonspecific answers or viewing them as indicators
that you have begun to nudge a responsive chord.

    YOU: Shall we see if we can't work out a compromise?
    ABBY: What's that?
    YOU: That's when two people sit down to work out their
          problems to see if they can't find a way so that both
          people will be satisfied. We want you to get enough
          sleep and you want to stay up late. Now, we can't
          agree to letting you stay up a whole hour later, but
          maybe part of it would be okay.
    ABBY: How much?
    YOU: That depends on what you're willing to do.

and so forth . . . keeping in mind that what lies under the
whole exchange is most likely a question of attention and
love.

    We'll admit that, for the purposes of our discussion, Abby
is a fairly clear-cut child. In the heat of real life things get
more complicated. The point is to *keep your own mind simple;* don't get caught up in the side issues, the false issues, the
brickbats. The more simply you can visualize the events, the
better off you will be. Don't allow yourself to be waylaid by
noticing that Abby's pajamas have a spot of dessert on the

front. You're dealing with the love/TV/Louise syndrome now, not with the fact that Abby's table manners offend your delicate sensibilities! As soon as you shift ground on the child, you screw everything up: "I want to watch TV." "What's that on your pajama top?" "Jello. Can I watch?" "You're such a slob . . ." That's not compromise; it's madness.

Maybe you have no children or you have perfect children and you are wondering what Abby and her Dr. Dentons have to do with your life. Take any conflict situation and the players can look an awful lot like Abby and her parents. In each of the following instances the victim chose, incorrectly, to fight back:

> WIFE: You never pay any attention to me. Fred's wife always gets attention from Fred.
> HUSBAND: Why are you wearing that awful bathrobe?

> BOSS: Are you sure you're doing the best you can?
> EMPLOYEE: I sure am! I work twice as hard as anyone else around here!

> TWIN 1: You better stop trying to steal my girlfriends.
> TWIN 2: I wouldn't try to steal those dogs!

In each of these cases Fighting Back (triangle) is an inappropriate response, because not one of the attacks offers a win/lose situation or contest as we've defined it. You can't measure attention; you can't measure maximum output on the job; and you can't measure loyalty. These clearly are no-win situations which could best be responded to by Parleying—by being a circle of compromise.

HUSBAND: Let's see if we can't iron out the problem about attention. I'm sorry it's bothering you. I have a lot on my mind, but we should be able to figure something out. I do love you.

EMPLOYEE: If you feel I'm not putting out my best work, let's take a look at my workload and see where we can juggle it a bit.

TWIN 2: I enjoy talking to your girlfriends. Maybe we can figure a way that'll increase the trust that seems to have gone down the tubes around here.

In each of these conflicts there is probably truth on both sides which needs to be explored and resolved harmoniously. Notice that none of the responders gave up and played dead. They approached the point of the attack head on and Parleyed, rather than Fighting Back or Withdrawing.

Of course, if your adversary continues to rant and rave, you may, after a fair hearing, be forced to try another conflict response. As we said, Parley requires *two* circles.

As a response to conflict, Parley must be used with the proper spirit—as with all the Attack-tics responses— with confidence and a reaching out to encompass the attack. It is not to be thought of as a gimmick or as a way of trading your fear for a moment's peace. Parley is a meeting of equal minds and hearts, not a venture into sleight of hand. It must spring from your sincere desire to solve a problem, and not just be a way of winning something you didn't have before. *Stay balanced, don't play games, and focus on the problem, not the opponent. Don't worry about your ego. It'll be fine!*

4. DOING NOTHING

Doing Nothing can be a delightful experience on a hot summer's day, and it can also be the best response to some events of conflict. In the Attack-tics system, Doing Nothing is represented by a square.

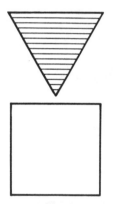

When you think about the square as a geometric form, you will begin to see that Doing Nothing in the face of conflict is not the same thing as giving up or being passive. A square is a solid form, well grounded, like the triangle, and capable of withstanding a great deal of pressure. Its strength is its solidity. Its weakness is its inability to move fluidly. For years we've all talked about people as "squares" without understanding how right we were. The square is usually inflexible, unwilling or unable to change with the flow of life around him or her. By the same token, the square is dependable and trustworthy. We talk about "square deals" and know that we're fully protected.

Thus, Doing Nothing is not to be confused with giving up or letting the world ride roughshod over you. Like all the other responses, it is appropriate or inappropriate depending completely on the circumstance.

How can Doing Nothing ever be the right response?

Take the following example: You come home to your house or your apartment. To the best of your knowledge, you locked the door when you left, and nobody else has had access to your place during your absence. Nevertheless, the front door is slightly ajar.

If you're alarmed, if you're a cop, if you're suicidal, you might leap inside like something out of a marine corps training exercise, screaming karate yells and behaving like the cavalry.

If you're still with us and reasonably reasonable, you might find it best to wait a few minutes (depending on the situation) to see what develops. This extra time could reveal whether a friend you forgot about is inside, the house is occupied by felons, or you simply didn't lock the door properly.

While Doing Nothing you have one great advantage: You can think about what to do next—call the police, call a neighbor, go inside, or whatever. The important point to bear in mind is that the Doing Nothing stage is a genuine, useful response to that event.

The same process applies in interpersonal conflict. You can Do Nothing. It is your right, and in many instances it is the best thing to do.

WHEN TO DO NOTHING

Doing Nothing is appropriate when you need time. Time to figure out what's coming at you and why, time to establish a response pattern, time to establish a sense of priorities, time to ask yourself all the questions which Attack-tics demands.

There seems to us to be an inordinate premium placed on quick responses. That's what the average attacker plans on. Your friend yells and you yell back. Your boss yells and you cringe instantly. In short, the attacker has chosen the time and place and also dictates the rhythm of the conflict. Attackers count on your dancing to their metronome, so your refusal to do that can be a highly effective response.

Doing Nothing is an appropriate response when you want to find out what's really going on behind the attack. Because the attacker is a triangle coming at you, he or she is committed to a single point. Attackers find it hard to stop. If you Do Nothing, say nothing, many times they will continue full speed ahead, awkwardly blurting out the truth. For example:

ARTHUR: Dammit, Peg, I'm sick and tired of always having to call you!

PEG: (Waits, says nothing, watches Arthur.)

ARTHUR: I mean, how do you think it makes me feel?

PEG: (Ditto from above.)

ARTHUR: I'm about to give up on you completely.

PEG: (Ditto.)

ARTHUR: I mean, I really do love you, you know. But I don't like always having to be the one who makes all the overtures.

PEG: (Ditto.)

ARTHUR: (Softer.) Don't you love me a little bit?

PEG: I love you, Arthur. Let's see if we can't work this out . . .

Peg does nothing until Arthur has exhausted his attack and declared that, contrary to being sick and tired, he's really just trying to get Peg's love. From that moment on they can move back to compromise, Parley, and find a resolution to the conflict. The important thing is that Peg didn't do what most of us do: Fight Back.

ARTHUR: Dammit, Peg, I'm sick and tired of always having to call you!

PEG: Oh, come off it, Arthur, I call you just as much as you call me!

ARTHUR: You do not! All last week I had to call you.

PEG: Well, I can't be expected to run around calling everybody all the time! I've got a life to lead too, you know!

ARTHUR: You're so selfish!

PEG: You're egotistical!

And before the sun sets on Arthur and Peg's ex-relationship, they're locked in one of life's most irreversible conflicts.

The thing to remember is there is no rule that says that every thrust requires a parry or riposte. *You don't have to answer charges all your life.*

You are better that that.

Doing Nothing is one of the best responses of all when an attack makes no sense, when it is totally absurd. Rather than dignify the attack by reacting, you Do Nothing.

How many times have we inadvertently angered some cuckoo behind the wheel of another car? We waited too long at a green light, took somebody else's lane in traffic, looked sideways, breathed out backward, or committed one of a million slights that zanies find exasperating.

What happens next? The zany yells at us, insults us, implies horrendous things about our heritage, our face, mental state, etc.

Unless he or she is bearing down on us in an eighteen-wheel truck, the best response is none whatsoever. With any luck the crazy will conclude that we're hard of hearing or incurably stupid and move away. And away is the very best, warmest, friendliest place to be when crazies are angry.

But what usually happens? The zany makes a verbal lunge: "You idiot! Where'd you get your driver's license, Sears, Roebuck?"

And we lunge back. Lord knows why. We feel almost compelled to respond. We feel small. Injured. We feel he's getting away with something. Maybe we want to justify our driving error: "I learned to drive at the Creedmoor Driving Institute and got high honors, you jerk!"

All that and we keep telling our children that "sticks and stones may break your bones, but names will never harm you." No wonder kids are confused! We tell them one thing, and as soon as some nut blows his horn at us or calls us a name, we sally forth with all our brilliance.

Remember, a loony-tunes attack yelled from a passing car is a serious attack only if you decide to make it so. If you pick up the gauntlet, you've given the attack far more importance than it deserves.

To recap: In order to use Doing Nothing as an effective response to conflict, the first step is to get over any lingering doubts you may have about your bravery or lack of it. Remember, you *choose* to Do Nothing. You don't Do Nothing because you're afraid to do something. And you don't lose face if you know inside that the choice to Do Nothing was your own. If anything, you feel healthier, wholer, and prepared for whatever the next stage of the conflict might be . . . if there is any.

5. DECEPTION

When Deception is used in the Attack-tics spirit, it is a legitimate protective response to attack.

As in the case of Withdrawal, it's crucial that we divest the word of its accrued values. Certainly we do not envision a world based on deception, nor are we encouraging you to become oily benders of truth and goodness. What we want is for you to see Deception as a means of deflecting or redirecting an attack. It is neither good nor bad. It can be both.

For example, who can fault the woman who, according to newspaper accounts of a few years ago, told a would-be rapist that she had venereal disease and if he knew what was good for him he'd try his luck elsewhere? That was a clear case of Deception that even the most self-righteous would not quibble with.

Who can fault the parent who, when a child is close to breaking an heirloom, distracts the little one with a quick dose of "Look, Lucy, see the bird outside the window?" Whether the scarlet tanager is there or not, the transaction is Deceptive because the parent is not really interested in the bird so much as in the porcelain statue of the little French maid.

Thus, Deception is used all the time to deflect and redirect someone from a potential disaster. In the Attack-tics system, Deception is, as one might imagine, represented by a shaded circle:

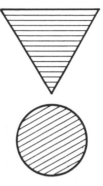

Neither solid like the square, nor purely directed like the triangle, the circle allows you to spin your attacker around —using a ploy. As in Parley, you enter into some kind of discussion with the attacker, but Deception adds the element of untruth.

In essence, Deception buys time; it does not settle issues of conflict. As soon as the parent decides that birds outside the window have solved the problem with the porcelain statue, the child is off to smash the glass unicorn. Deception saved the statue; it's now up to the parent to solve the overall problem of breakable objects and a curious child. In the same way, the woman who held off the rapist with a lie about venereal disease is still stuck with the fact that she was at the wrong place at the wrong time, regardless of her right to personal safety. Reality, for what it's worth, demands that she reorganize her approach to her environment as it exists or change that environment. Otherwise, she'll be trying the same lie over and over again.

Therefore, Deception (and its partner, surprise) is for buying time, not for solving problems.

KINDS OF DECEPTION

In essence, Deception as a conflict response comes in two basic forms: diversion and deflection.

Diversion: Putting Up a Smokescreen

Diversion" simply means getting the attacker off his or her original mission by surprising him or her and offering something else to look at. It ranges from the mother saying "Look at the bird" to your asking your angry mother how her sinuses are when she wants to tell you what a louse you are for not writing often enough. The sharp attacker may well come back with a "Don't change the subject," but you're well within your rights to continue the diversions and keep them coming. After all, you're only trying to buy time until the attacker gives up or a better strategy comes to you.

Deflection: The White Lie

In its simplest form, deflection is telling an outright lie: "I would have called earlier but my insurance man came over and I couldn't get rid of him." The extremity of the lie depends on your own creativity and the severity of the conflict. For example, in a fairly low-level conflict you can go cautiously or you can go whole hog, hoping the attacker will see the absurdity of his attack:

A: You forgot to call me! What the hell happened?
B: I'm really sorry.
A: That's no excuse!
B: I would have called you, but I was attacked by Martians from outer space who wanted to drag me off in their capsule!

A: That's absurd!

B: I know. So is continuing to rage at somebody after they've said they're sorry.

WHEN TO USE DECEPTION

When the time and place are wrong, Deception can be your best option. "Don't start up with me, Harold, I've got people coming over in two minutes and they wouldn't want to see us fighting." Granted, she hasn't stopped Harold in the ultimate scheme of things, but she has bought time—time during which Harold *may* cool down.

Deception can be best employed *when you want to surprise an opponent,* break his line of intention, or catch him off guard. Most attacks, as we've seen, come right at you along a fairly straight line. By employing Deception (surprise) you can break that line and cause the attack to misfire.

Let's say that you're a business executive who receives the following phone call:

> ATTACKER: Listen, you! I'm fed up with your shenanigans, and I'm not about to put up with them any more!

The attacker is coming straight at you with all his stops out. That sometimes makes it easy for you to break his intention by coming up with a surprise of your own:

> YOU: Hang on, Frank. I've got a call on the other line. Let me get rid of him.

With that you put him on Hold and do what one executive (who's practiced Attack-tics for some years now) does: get up and get a drink of water, practice a few golf swings, cool off and give your attacker a chance to cool down. Even if the attacker is angrier after his wait, you are in a better position to handle his attack, because now you're ready for it. You've combined Deception with another response—Withdrawal.

While we're at it, you can also combine Deception with Fighting Back. A friend of ours, a relatively easygoing man, became very nervous when he was wrongfully stopped by a traffic cop. The cop had obviously had a bad day, and his perceptions were way off. He began screaming at our friend about his flagrant disregard for life and safety and limb. Our friend relaxed as much as he could under the circumstances, realizing, because of his Attack-tics training, that Fighting Back or Withdrawing would be the worst choice he could make. The policeman was obviously in no mood to Parley. Doing Nothing until the storm had passed over was possible, but what then?

As soon as the cop stopped long enough to catch his breath, our friend looked up intently and said, "Officer, you can't talk to me this way! I'm a Scoutmaster in Detroit!"

The lie was so off the wall and illogical that the policeman stopped dead in his tracks and let our friend off with a mild warning. The cop thought he'd done a good deed, and our friend had given the cop a chance to feel better about himself. Harmony.

In another situation, Chick, Eileen's ex-husband, upon learning that she had broken up with her new boyfriend, called her and said: "I hope you know what it feels like to get dumped. I hope you know the pain you made me feel." In actuality, Eileen was having a very nice time with her new freedom, and at first she fought back, telling Chick that she was not feeling all the pain he hoped she was. That only encouraged Chick to keep on calling. Finally she tried Deception. She "admitted" that she really was miserable—

and she didn't stop there. She went on to tell Chick in lavish detail how miserable she was. Every time Chick tried to interrupt, she went on about a new fit of depression, another bout with suicide. It got to the point where Chick finally said, "I'm sorry, Eileen. I guess it's tough all over."

"Yes, Chick. Nobody has a corner on pain."

"I'm sorry I acted the way I did," Chick replied.

Eileen's Deception worked perfectly. It enabled Chick to confront his own anger, and made him begin to feel human again. A trick, perhaps—but it ended up being the solution to more than the problem of unwanted phone calls.

HOW TO USE DECEPTION

Deception need not be as outlandish as the "Scoutmaster's" or as poignant as Eileen's. In general, our best use of Deception occurs when we stay fairly believable and remember what it was that we said. Therefore, the best single rule for the use of Deception is: *Invent stories which have a grain of truth.*

The rest is up to you. You know your adversaries best. You know what you can bring yourself to do. Just remember that Deception is a response you make consciously, based on past experience and present problems. All Attack-tics asks is that you use it with a clear head and without fooling yourself into thinking that it offers a permanent solution.

Before taking you on to Attack-tics' very special and most effective conflict option—for which we have set aside an entire chapter—let's look back at how far we have come since Robin Hood and Little John confronted each other on the log.

We've discussed so far five different responses to conflict:

1. Fighting Back
2. Withdrawal
3. Parley
4. Doing Nothing
5. Deception

These are to be viewed as essentially independent responses, although you can mix and match them, as we've seen. Once you've selected one, you must always be prepared to shift gears and employ another if necessary. No single one of these five is best or worst—each depends upon the circumstances, the conflict, the attacker, the time, and the place.

The problem, as always, is managing your feelings in order to make what you consider rational choices based on your perception of all elements of the situation. Your success will lie in your ability to find your center and retain it, or regain it if it gets lost.

V

Centering

For the uncontrolled there is
no wisdom.
For the uncontrolled
no concentration.
For the unconcentrated
no peace.
For the unpeaceful
no happiness can be.

—*Bhagavad-Gita*

Balance.

It's all about balance. Our common speech is full of uses of the word and concept of balance. In front of our courts we have Roman or Greek ladies in diaphanous robes and blindfolds permanently holding balance scales just to show us that justice is evenhanded and fair. The lives of convicted killers and seriously ill patients are "hanging in the balance." One of our past Presidents was fond of saying (just before delivering a pronouncement) that "on balance" it looked as if taxes would go up. We admire the incredible sense of balance which Philippe Petit possessed on his high-wire walk between the towers of the World Trade Center. Football sportscasters speak about the "balanced offense," the "unbalanced line," and the balance required of an interior lineman. Ballet stars mystify their audiences by balancing on one toe and twirling endlessly. Our Olympic gymnastic teams even compete on a Robin Hood/Little John type of log called a "balance beam."

Our understanding of the word "balance" extends beyond what we sometimes call the purely physical. Somebody who's deranged may be called "unbalanced." Politicians call for a "balanced approach." When we've been caught by surprise and, usually, defeated, we say "I was off balance."

The strange thing is that nobody ever taught us that physical and emotional or spiritual balance are inextricably related. We've come down the philosophical pike believing that mind and matter, spirit and body, are separate entities. We see ourselves as split into two independent halves, each blaming the other for whatever goes wrong. "I wasn't concentrating, my mind was wandering, and I stumbled." "I tried to work out the answer, but I had a headache and couldn't think."

Why?

Why should we reintegrate and become *centered*, balanced? Very simply, because balance is the key to using any of the options discussed in this book. To Fight Back, Withdraw, Parley, Do Nothing, or Deceive while off balance would be as disastrous as facing the Assyrian hordes with a toothpick. Even more important, how can we reach any decision about the nature of a particular conflict and its appropriate response while we are off balance? Throughout the previous chapter we told you that your choices must be made as objectively and rationally as possible. To do that you must be on balance.

The nice thing about balance, we've found, is that when

you take a physically balanced position your mind and spirit come into balance as well. Likewise, if your body is off balance you can regain your equilibrium almost as easily by reaching a balanced state inside your mind.

It works. The problem is in maintaining that balance in the midst of a furor over who had the car keys last, who lost the rent check, who spilled the soup, who burned the grits, or who insulted whom first. That takes practice—enough practice so that balance, both internal and external, functions independently of your will.

Centering is the act of achieving balance. We'll show you how to get there. Then, staying centered is up to you.

Why do we use the term "centering" to describe balance? Think of the potter at his wheel. He has a lump of clay and a spinning disk on which he hopes to create an elegant pot. If he tosses the clay anywhere but dead center, his pot will be thrown across the room, ending up like a kindergartener's ashtray . . . if he's lucky. It takes hundreds of failures for an amateur potter to learn how to use his materials and his machine so that he will be able to get to the part where he makes delicate flares—in short, to where he can begin to create.

Martial artists have spent at least a thousand years studying the art of balance, not only to increase their skills with sword, bow and arrow, and so forth, but also to enable them to meet life and its conflicts in a relaxed but alert manner. They cannot face an oncoming swordsman while hysterical and off balance, any more than we can face an irate friend while our center of gravity is somewhere above our left eyebrow.

In Attack-tics, as in Aikido, your main balance point or center of gravity is located approximately two inches below your navel. Called the *tantien,* or "one-point," this center is where you should be living, whether you are under attack or just watching the flowers grow. It is the junction of time and space, it is a reservoir of calm, it is an "organ" which can sense attack faster than the intellect—it is what we sometimes call (because nobody ever taught us about it) "the pit of the stomach." If we listen to it, we'll be better protected than if we hired a part-time bodyguard.

The center, the one-point, is not shown on the average anatomy chart in American medical texts. If it'll make you feel better, you're perfectly free to think of it as an imaginary spot. The center will work for you no matter what you think it is. It's not mystical. It just works.

To get and hold your center, to experience what we're talking about, first lie comfortably with your back against the floor and relax all your muscles. Don't try to hold yourself in any position. Let your body find its own relaxed state. Pay attention to your breathing. Don't push it, just let it slow down and regulate itself.

Now place your hand on your center, your one-point, approximately two inches below your navel. Relax and gradually let your concentration be on that spot where your hand is resting. Imagine that all your focus, all your energy, is coming down from your forehead (where most of us live), down from your chest (where we imprison most of our energy), and into that spot. Again, pay attention to your breathing to make sure that the effort of lowering your concentration hasn't become too strained.

Once you begin to feel that you are succeeding, that your focus has arrived in your center, concentrate on keeping it there. If it helps you, visualize that spot and imagine that your eyes have become relocated there. What you should begin to feel when you are centered is a further relaxation of all your muscles, especially your shoulders and chest. You may notice a sensation of warmth which spreads down your thighs and legs, relaxing those muscles. Unless you've taken the relaxation part too seriously and dozed off, you will also notice a heightened awareness of yourself in space and time. In effect, you have returned to yourself and are one with the moment.

Practice locating your one-spot for ten to fifteen minutes a day. If nothing else happens for you as a result of Attacktics, your cardiologist will appreci the extra relaxation you're giving your heart. As you become more comfortable with the idea and with that part of your body, begin to gain your center without the use of your hand. Simply concentrate on the spot, feel it warm up as you get into it, and hold it. If your mind slips off into worries and fears, don't push it; gradually allow your center to reassert itself. Try not to tense up with each minor failure of concentration. You'll get it back, and soon those interruptions will be fewer and fewer.

There's no way to say how long this overall process should take. Those of you who have had some experience with yoga or t'ai chi will be able to do it faster. Others may take longer. Nobody can fail at it unless he or she gives up. Your one-spot is your center, and everybody has one.

The next step in the process of centering is to begin to experiment with finding and holding your center while sitting or standing. The act is the same—there are just more distractions than when you were lying on the floor. If you are sitting, imagine that the one-spot has real weight; when you lower your concentration, allow yourself to feel heavier, sinking farther and farther into your chair. Adopt a relaxed and alert posture and sink down.

Next, try to center while in a standing position. Stand with one foot slightly forward of the other—if you're right-handed, you'll be more comfortable with the left foot forward; if you're left-handed, slide your right foot forward. Experiment until you find a comfortable position, with your weight evenly distributed on both feet and your knees very slightly bent to absorb your weight and allow you to move quickly. The advancement of the front foot will turn your body slightly away from dead center; in the martial arts this turn of the body offers an attacker a smaller target, and that's not a bad idea when you are involved in any face-to-face encounter where conflict is possible. You don't offer your full front to an angry enemy.

When you've become comfortable in this stance—and it is difficult at first, because we're so used to locking our knees and standing flat-footed with our feet next to each other— you can repeat the centering process, lowering your concentration, moving it down to the floor and even through the floor. Remind your other muscles not to tense up; stand easily and comfortably, keeping your center.

An excellent way to test the effect of your centering is to ask a friend to help. First, imagine that your center is at the top of your head. Place all your concentration there and think upward. Then, while standing, have a friend lift you into the air. He or she can grasp you from behind and lift up from the waist, or push upward under your arms.

The next step is to ground yourself, center, and think downward. Even go so far as to imagine that your feet have grown roots into the floor. Now ask your friend to lift you. If you've concentrated and kept your center while being lifted, the friend should notice a dramatic difference in your apparent weight. Proficient students of martial arts can even get to the higher point where no one can budge them off the floor; we have seen weightlifters strain at lifting an eighty-five-pound person!

Nobody's quite sure why this phenomenon works. It really doesn't matter. The grounded, centered person cannot be budged, and yet he or she can move quickly and sense danger better than the ungrounded, uncentered person. Just as important, grounded, centered people appear different from the other kind; attackers seem to sense their stability, and pick on other people rather than confront those who live in their one-spot.

When you've gained some experience in centering, you can start to hold it while moving, walking, playing tennis, dancing, or driving down the highway. Depending on the activity, imagine that you are led forward in space by a string attached to your center. It's hard at first, but begin by trying it while walking down the sidewalk, pulled along from your center. Very quickly you'll discover that you're making much more solid contact with the pavement, your feet stay close to the earth, you have a better sense of balance. As we noted earlier, you should also find that your attitude is much calmer, that you feel less scattered and more competent to deal with whatever happens along the way. It is precisely this feeling we're working for in Attack-tics. In any conflict, whether you are walking, sitting, standing, or running, the centered attitude is the one which maximizes your chances for making the right choices, for responding successfully, for surviving in the best, most harmonious way. If you carry yourself from your center, people will not stare at you on the street or wonder who the weirdo is. It's a normal gait, and needn't be exaggerated for effect unless you're practicing. Keep reminding yourself to keep your center. You'll find it wanders on occasion, but you should be able to regain it with a minimum of effort.

The real test of your newly developed skill will come when you are tired, irritable, or, most crucially, in conflict. Fear can often send your concentration and energy right up through your chest, into your throat, and out the top of your head. Your breath stops momentarily, and all those marvelously relaxed muscles go right into spasms of tension. When the boss yells at you or someone insults you, you must pay primary attention to restoring your center, not to striking back or running like a dervish. Sure, you'll lose it. Survival depends on your getting it back quickly.

For contrast, let's see what normally happens to the un-centered person. The energy and concentration shoot up-ward, sometimes lodging in the muscles where the neck and shoulders are joined. This upward thrust pulls the person off-balance physically, and, simultaneously, the spirit and intellect are dislodged. He stammers or trips while trying to escape, and has a good chance of being caught one way or another. He'll stumble physically, or create some inane rea-sons for his exit, or trap himself in an intellectual maze. We've all experienced getting caught and having to invent excuses right and left, only a few of which make sense: "I would have done it right away, sir, but my, uh, my, uh, my mother was, er, uh, taken to the hospital and I had to be by her bedside . . ." Five minutes later your mother walks in and your lie comes apart like a dollar watch. TV's situation comedies are built around characters being off center! Your ability to harmonize and survive depends on exactly the opposite.

Let's suppose you're a salesperson behind a counter. You're going along, holding your balance, keeping your cen-ter, and doing okay. A customer comes along, and your center signals you that something's not right. But before your mind can assess the situation, the customer is all over you, yelling about this or claiming that. Your center gets lost in the shuffle, and your mind, now off balance, begins madly to think up all those put-downs you remember from Don Rick-les or your grammar-school teacher: "Listen, mister, if brains were dynamite you couldn't blow your nose!" Fortu-nately, you keep your cliché to yourself, even though your eyes are burning and you feel what you consider to be a legitimate urge to kill. Instead, you shift your weight and come back to balance, turning your body slightly, unlocking your knees, and finding your center. You check your breathing to slow it from the hysterical puffing that adrenaline seems to demand. Now you can handle it. You listen to what's going on, assess the situation on the basis of everything you've learned thus far, and make your choice or choices. You find a way to help the irate customer regain his own balance, calm down, and rejoin the human race with you. You give him the gift of harmony.

So it's okay to lose your balance—temporarily. All the shifts and reshifts of balance in the preceding scene take place in less than a second once you get good at it. And when you get really proficient you stay centered no matter what.

It's all about balance, whether in diet or soul or body. They're all the same, anyway.

VI

Aiki

We know that human society is built on the foundation of this bond (love and friendship), but we have to recognize the fact that the bond has become too limited to encompass all that it should: It prevents aggression only between those who know each other and are friends, while obviously it is all active hostility between all men of all nations or ideologies that must be stopped. the obvious conclusion is that love and friendship should embrace all humanity, that we should love all our human brothers indiscriminately.

—Konrad Lorenz
On Aggression

In Harper Lee's novel *To Kill a Mockingbird,* Atticus tells his children that you never really know anybody until you've "walked around in his skin" for a while. He never limited that statement by saying, "You walk around only in nice people's skin." He meant everybody.

A popular Native American poem says much the same thing, making the point that "you can't know me until you've walked a mile in my moccasins." That sentiment was country-and-westernized in a song entitled "Walk a Mile in My Shoes."

In its simplest form, that is the essence of Aiki, the sixth and, to us, the most effective response to conflict. It is also the most difficult to learn.

Certainly it's a whole lot easier to walk a mile in a nice comfy pair of loafers than it is in a set of jackboots. It is easier and more pleasant to understand peaceful, humane folks than it is to harmonize with bullies, neurotics, and the off-balance folk of this world. But, significantly, one of the best ways to survive and "win" with the unpleasant people is to do just that. Flow with them. Harmonize.

"You mean you want me to join with the bad guys?"

In a very special sense, yes. That doesn't mean you're going to be asked to join your mugger and help him mug yourself, or become a mugger in your spare time. You'll see later how it's different from "If you can't beat 'em, join 'em."

An old Japanese expression goes: "Be the water, not the rock." That too is the essence of Aiki. Picture a stream chuckling along within its banks. A large dark rock stands right smack in the middle of the stream. That's how most of us deal with life and conflict. We are like that large dark rock. Like King Canute, we put out our hands and yell for the waters to stop. But the water keeps churning and flowing along, bouncing off us, streaming around us and over us. The water has direction and flexibility. Eon by eon the rock is worn down, until halfway through eternity it has become a pebble.

And that's what happens to us some days, isn't it? Conflict, fights, squabbles, disagreements, insults—the entire catechism of stress and anguish. By the time we've gotten home we've become pebbles. We curse ourselves, we shrivel up, and we die just a little bit.

But what would happen if that rock could turn? At the very least it would stand a chance of surviving longer. As the water struck it, the rock would swivel around in the direction it was pushed. (Don't start fretting about the fact that there would be friction on its base, wearing it down; this is only a metaphor.) If the rock could turn with the force of the water, still retaining its place in the stream bed, the rock would lose nothing; the water would continue past.

That is part of the spirit of Aiki.

There is an old tale—no one quite knows where it originated—which tells of the solid oak tree which stands next to the slender reed. The oak boasts of its strength, insulting the reed's delicacy—until the typhoon hits. The oak's inability to bend causes its destruction. It is uprooted by the wind and flattened. The reed holds its ground by flowing with the wind, letting it blow itself far out to sea.

That is part of the spirit of Aiki.

When you step out of a building on a windy day and are caught full force, you don't have to think about turning your body away from the wind to protect your eyes from the flying cinders. You simply go with it, spinning around on your feet so that you're facing away from the onslaught.

That is also part of the spirit of Aiki.

There was once a man of great strength who, for his own reasons, engaged in a fight with a revolving door, determined to win in this great contest. He walked up to it and pushed with all his might. The door made three full revolutions before it came to rest again. He pushed even harder, and the door swung around four times. In desperation, the strong man got inside the revolving door and pushed and pushed, running as fast as he could to keep from being smacked by the door that followed him around and around. As onlookers gaped they saw the strong man run faster and faster, until finally the centrifugal force he had created tossed him back out onto the street in a heap. Frustrated and angry, he picked himself up and walked over to a conventional locked door which sported every known security device on its steel casing. In a few seconds he'd knocked down the door and derived some consolation from his victory. Some of the on-lookers who'd watched decided that the conventional door needed stronger dead-bolts and five heavy-duty brass hinges. Others cheered the revolving door but lamented the fact that it still let people in. A few suggested that the strong man might do well to increase his protein intake. A small boy looked at the whole situation and smiled.

Be the water, not the rock.

The revolving door's appointed task was not to keep people out or bar their way. It was to welcome them in. It gave nothing up, nor did it loose its ground or compromise its ideals. The strong man, in his anger, destroyed himself by pushing harder and running harder while the revolving door only accommodated his wish to go faster.

We can choose to be the revolving door and welcome in even the strongest, most off-balanced of mankind, or we can put more locks on ourselves, learn boxing, invent strangleholds, carry tear gas in our purses, yell louder, and stand more resolutely.

Be the water, not the rock.

In the Attack-tics system, Aiki is designated by a solid circle. (Later we'll see that the circle does not tell the whole story, but for now, begin to feel the circularity of the response.)

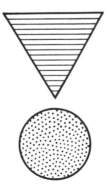

Like the revolving door, the circle accepts the attack and turns with it, letting the point of the triangle or the brunt of the attack pass on in the direction it has chosen.

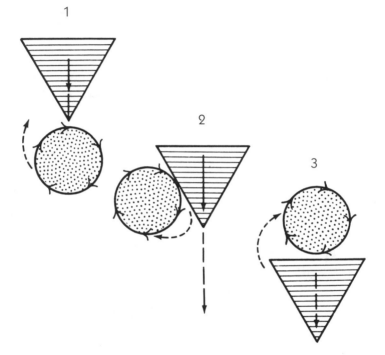

By position 3, the attacker has gone on by and the responder is in the rather safe position behind him.

You see, that's the nice thing about sincere, focused attacks: They are so clearly directed at that point of the triangle, so committed to destroying you that they develop their own momentum and energy. That momentum will carry them past you if you roll or turn at the right moment. If you turn too early, your attacker will spot your response and change course. If you turn too late, you'll end up with the tip of the triangle sticking in your center.

If an attack is insincere and unfocused, if the attacker is only halfhearted about it, you don't have to do anything anyway. Nobody ever got hurt by a halfhearted attack except the attacker.

So that you don't confuse Aiki with Deception, bear in mind that the circle *accepts* the attack. By the time the attacker reaches position 2 in the preceding diagram both the attacker and the responder are facing in the same direction. It is at that point that the responder, you, begins to empathize, begins to walk around in the attacker's skin, begins to understand the reasons behind the attack. It may seem complicated at this point, but remember that being a circle requires that you are not just a slippery person, but that you are engaging in a relationship with the person who is trying to attack you.

To remove this view from the geometrical and give it a human dimension, picture the following situation: You are standing comfortably centered and someone pushes you on the right shoulder with his right hand. You resist the temptation to make your right shoulder rigid; instead, turning from your one-point, your center, you accept his push and turn with it. If the friend continues to push in the direction he's chosen, he should end up across the room and out of your way. Partway through the move you will have noticed that the two of you are standing shoulder to shoulder (your left, his right) and looking in the direction of his push. This is one of the most important moments in Attack-tics. In metaphorical terms, it means that you are now in a position to understand what he's up to, but you're also in a position of safety. You gave nothing up, you can walk around in his shoes, and you are safe from his pushing until he redirects his next lunge. And yet, if the two of you are in harmony, shoulder to shoulder, you are also in a good position to redirect his drive and his energy. If it's a life-or-death situation, you can push him away and run. If it's a nonphysical situation, you can help him see how his behavior is hurting him.

It's worth repeating: 1) You accept the attack in a centered position. 2) You accept it in a centered position and turn from your center. 3) You harmonize and you redirect his attack. Keep your center at all times or you'll lose your balance, be unable to harmonize, and destroy whatever confluence could have developed.

Now, let's see what this looks like in social conflict, rather than physical conflict.

Patricia has problems with her parents. She's a member of a very big "club" of people who do. But knowing that doesn't always help her a great deal, because it always seems that when she wants most to love them and be loved by them, somebody (more often her mother, sad to say) picks a fight. Her mother is one of those people whom popular psychologists describe as a person who can't accept love and disguises her fear of rejection by rejecting first.

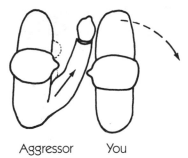

Figure 1

Aggressor   You

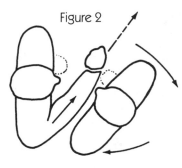

Figure 2

Aggressor   You

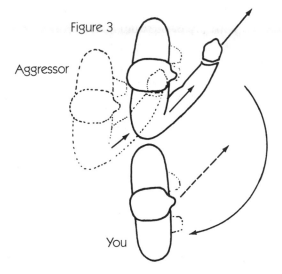

Figure 3

Aggressor

You

But Patricia isn't totally cool either. She is unsure of her own identity and still depends too much on her parents' approval. Again, knowing this hasn't helped Patricia all that much.

Her parents live in Florida, retired and, as things go in our economy, comfortable without being able to afford real luxuries. Patricia lives alone in an apartment in New York. At twenty-seven, she has done fairly well for herself as an assistant buyer for a department store, but she can't afford many luxuries either.

Late in the winter, Patricia gets the idea that she would like to visit her parents. She hasn't seen them in a year, and phone calls get so complicated sometimes. Moreover, the winter's been tough, and she thinks she deserves a week off. The airfare and her contribution to the food budget in Florida will leave her almost strapped, but certainly not so far in debt as to consider bankruptcy or streetwalking. In short, she'd like to visit her parents because she really does love them.

Perhaps Patricia is a mite off base in her expectations. She fantasizes that her offer/request to come south will be received with joy even though she knows nothing is ever easy with these two senior citizens.

She calls.

Almost as soon as her plan is out over the Bell System lines, her mother starts in.

> MOTHER: Patty, you can't afford to come all that long way down here! Do you have any idea what it costs? Good God, honey, isn't it about time you grew up and faced the fact that there isn't anybody who's gonna take care of you but you! When are you going to develop some little sense of reality? You'll never change. You and your father are cut out of the same piece of cloth. Spend, spend, spend!

You honestly think your father and I'd be living as we do if he'd saved just a little bit for the future? No ma'am! Come off it, Patty, and be reasonable. You've got to shape up now or you'll be hanging on by your fingernails for the rest of your life. You're not married, and who, may I ask is going to support you if you do dumb things like this all the time?

A quick analysis of the mother's tirade shows that she's a pretty good attacker. Sure, she's worried about her daughter. She's made that amply clear. But she's not satisfied treating Patricia like an adult and simply offering a little advice. She begins by calling Patricia by her baby name, "Patty," which Patricia's been trying to shake for years. She insults her level of maturity. She insults her grasp of reality. She insults Pat's father, and socks in a little guilt by association before finishing off with a jibe about her not being married.

Patricia feels—allows herself to feel—completely rejected by the nice mommy of her fantasy. Her whole body shrinks, her eyes begin to tear up, and she wants to scream.

Let's assume that Patricia is off balance—a pretty fair assumption—and reacts the way most of us do in situations like this. (Afterward we'll demonstrate the Aiki approach.) She instantly goes on the defensive, trying to be reasonable but raising her voice decibel by decibel. Halfway through she starts into the old historical material.

PATRICIA: You always, always, always treat me this way! You don't have any respect for me and you never did! Why can't I make a perfectly reasonable suggestion without getting trampled on?

You must admit that her mother is a pretty good fighter, even if winning the battle loses her the war. She's got Patricia completely off balance, making personal attacks and raging against the unjustice of it all. In fact, Patricia's angry Fighting Back gives her mother all the weapons she needs to really decimate her daughter. Now she can turn the tables and appear calm and reasonable.

> MOTHER: Now, Patty. Patricia, if you'd rather, you know that what you've just said was said in the heat of the moment. Your father and I have always loved you. If we advise you on certain things it is precisely because we do love you . . .

A few minutes later Patricia hangs up, a completely wasted and defeated person. It's hard to believe that this is the same young woman who spends all day making up thousand-dollar orders and running an office which is responsible for a million dollars' worth of purchases each year. She cries for close to half an hour, reverting back to twenty-two years ago, when she could only rock back and forth, suck her thumb, and twiddle her hair. An hour later, angry rather than sad, she calls up her best friend and rats on her mother, telling her friend what a miserable, rotten person her mother really is. And what a weakling her father is for not backing her up! An hour after that, Patricia feels guilty for being disloyal to her mother by confiding in her friend.

A seven-minute fight. Twenty-four hours or more worth of anger, guilt, and remorse.

And don't say it doesn't happen. It's happening right this minute. It may not be mother and daughter. But it's happening.

Okay now, let's see what might have occurred if only two things had been different: Patricia was on balance and centered, and Patricia used Aiki (confluence).

From the moment Patricia sits down and begins to dial her parents' number, she is conscious of centering herself. As she breathes out easily, her shoulders relax from the tension and anxiety of having to deal with these people. She loves them very much, but she also understands that they have their hangups, that they are overprotective, and that they really do love her in their own peculiar way.

As she hears the phone ring on the other end, Patricia reminds herself to stay on balance. Her mother starts in.

> MOTHER: Patty, you can't afford to come all that long way down here! Do you have any idea what it costs? Good God, honey, it's about time that you grew up and faced the fact that there isn't anybody who's gonna take care of you but you! When are you going to develop some little sense of reality?

And so on.

Patricia keeps her balance, waiting until her mother has run out of steam. (She is a square, if you will.) Patricia's response to her mother's push is the same as when you respond to a friend's pushing you on the shoulder: She turns with the blow, and is now facing the same way as her mother.

> PATRICIA: You really are worried about me, aren't you, Mother? I guess having a child must really make a parent worry, especially when they live so far away.
>
> MOTHER: Your father and I lose sleep sometimes worrying about how you're making out, whether you'll ever find yourself a husband . . .
>
> PATRICIA: I do too, Ma. It's hard for both of us.
>
> MOTHER: We never said life would be a cinch.

What Patricia has done so far is achieve harmony with her mother's attack. She hasn't said anything she doesn't believe, and she hasn't given an inch in terms of her worth or her goals. She's empathized with an older woman who really does worry about her. They are now shoulder to shoulder, and perhaps they can begin to deal with the problem of whether Patricia gets to Florida. Even if she doesn't, she may well get something far more valuable in the long run: an even and harmonious relationship with the people who love her the most.

Let's play out the scene with Patricia and her mother to see what can happen. They are now shoulder to shoulder, each speaking from her heart about how hard it is. Patricia can now direct or lead her mother to come to grips with what is at stake.

PATRICIA: No, you never did tell me life was a cinch, and you gave me a lot of really good advice along the way. Some I've been able to use, and it's helped me. Some I've been too thick to use sometimes, and it's hurt. You've been good parents to me, and I just wanted to say thanks. I miss you.

MOTHER: We miss you too. I'm sorry we ended up so far away.

PATRICIA: Are you enjoying yourselves?

MOTHER: It's up and down. Your father troubles me a lot. He hasn't been feeling too well lately.

PATRICIA: I'm sorry. That must put a big strain on you.

MOTHER: Yes, sometimes.

PATRICIA: I guess daughters worry about their parents as much as parents worry about their daughters.

MOTHER: I guess. (Pause.) Look, honey, I'm sorry about flying off the handle a few minutes ago. I guess I've got a lot on my mind. We'd like to see you, but the money problems scare me so much these days.

PATRICIA: Mom, I love you both. How about if I don't buy
that fur coat I wanted so I can afford to come
down? I checked into the night-coach fares, so I
can cut the expense down to the bone.

MOTHER: If you really think it's okay.

PATRICIA: Thanks, Ma.

We want to call your attention to the pause which the
mother takes just before changing her mind, just before
apologizing. In the physical realm of martial arts there is
always that brief moment when, because of the defender's
response, the attacker loses his balance. *At that precise moment, the defender is in charge and must take care of the
attacker, helping him to a new, firmer, less aggressive balance.*
In our experience, in the nonphysical realm that loss of
balance is usually heralded by a pause. You must learn to
listen carefully for that pause. When it comes, take care of
your attacker. Lead him to harmony. Notice that when her
mother paused, Patricia then forgave her and helped restore
her mother's balance. She told her she loved her.

That's Aiki. Confluence. Flowing-with. Being the water
and not the rock.

It doesn't always work that easily; it would be less than
ethical to promise that it will. But Patricia used Aiki well.
She didn't lose her center and she didn't become embroiled
in an argument about whether or not she was a grown-up.
She didn't lie or dissemble. Perhaps she may have experienced a brief desire to give up along the way, but she held
on because, as we said up front, she does love her parents no
matter how exasperating they sometimes are. And, in the
long run, Patricia got much more than a week in Florida.

This last and best response to conflict is so foreign to
most of you that we're going to spend a great deal of
time discussing it, and we'll provide as many examples as
we can so that you can begin to try it out yourselves. At

first you'll balk. You'll accuse us of painting Pollyanna pictures of interpersonal relationships. We can take it; we're used to it at this stage in the Attack-tics process. Gradually, you'll move out, bite down your idea that Attack-tics is for sissies, and realize that it might just be a good thing to live in harmony with nature and your fellow man for a change.

The two key words that will be most helpful to you in the use of Aiki are "confluence" and "lead." Used in order, these separate actions will help you solve an amazing number of problems.

CONFLUENCE

First you must *join* with your attacker. Get alongside him or her. Agree with his right to feel whatever it is he's feeling. You're not necessarily agreeing with him about everything, but it certainly won't cost you anything to empathize. Become confluent. After all, he may be in the wrong, but you can't argue with the obvious fact that he is upset. Everyone is entitled to *feel*. And yet so often we *do* question or deny someone else's feelings.

> SON: You never save any dessert for me! I hate you!
> MOTHER: No you don't.
> SON: Yes, I do hate you! You never save me any ice cream! I hate you, I hate you, I hate you!
> MOTHER: How dare you hate your mother!
> SON: I hate you!

This sounds like it's part of a script that belongs off-off-off-Broadway, but you've undoubtedly witnessed (or, worse, participated in) fights just like that one. Or these:

LOVER #1: I don't love you any more.
LOVER #2: You can't mean that!

BOSS: I'm not happy with your work.
SECRETARY: How can that be? I stayed late all last week to finish that report.

STUDENT: This subject bores the hell out of me!
TEACHER: How could it be? French is the most beautiful language in the entire world.

PRODUCER: Your screenplay is rotten!
WRITER: You don't really believe that!

For the sake of argument, let's agree that all the first speakers in those little playlets were wrong. The mother only rarely ran out of ice cream; Lover #1 really *does* still love Lover #2; the boss is only confused and doesn't know what good work really is; the student adores French but wants attention from the teacher; and the producer wouldn't know a good screenplay from a rotten one. All of that is totally irrelevant to the fact that each of those attackers actually does *feel* what he or she says—at least consciously. What's going on subconsciously is, of course, another story.

It wouldn't take a genius from Vienna to postulate that the boss might want his secretary to bargain for her job with some Congressional-type favors between a couple of martinis. It's just as possible that Lover #1 is looking for some extra affection, to be seduced back into the relationship. The producer may be deliberately provoking the writer to defend his script. Or he might want to be convinced because he's insecure about his own judgment.

But none of this armchair analysis matters in the initial stage of confluence. You must begin where the attacker *says* he or she is, not where you *think* he or she is. It's *not* confluence to look smugly at your producer and say, "You're just saying my work is poor because you've always wanted to be a writer yourself!" It is most assuredly *NOT* confluence to tell your boss, "Yes, you *do* like my work; you're just mad about not getting a raise and you want me to feel bad so I'll mother you!" *Even if it's true!*

Remember, any underlying problems that exist can be dealt with only when the attacker himself can visualize them. Your job is to help him get there. This is how you do it:

SON: You never save any dessert for me! I hate you!
MOTHER: I'll bet that doesn't feel very good.

LOVER #1: I don't love you any more!
LOVER #2: I'm not the easiest person in the world to live with or love, am I.

BOSS: I'm not happy with your work!
SECRETARY: I don't blame you.

STUDENT: This subject bores the hell out of me.
TEACHER: Sometimes being a student is the pits.

PRODUCER: Your screenplay is rotten!
WRITER: First drafts never are perfect, are they.

In each case the second speaker made as genuine an effort as possible to see the situation from the opposite point of view. He did not give in. The first move is to the side, confluent with the attacker. Almost invariably, because an attacker is ipso facto off balance, this first response creates a kind of havoc in the attacker's mind, a special kind of imbalance, accompanied by that pause we discussed earlier. Most attackers are spoiling for a fight. They are overextended, and they need the victim to Fight Back and preserve their tenuous balance. So if you yell at a yeller, you help him stay upright.

LEAD

What most often precedes this point is the pause. This occurs when the attacker is trying to make sense out of what's just happened. The object of the attack can then remain silent or begin to lead. Let's take two of the previous examples and play them through to see this second process at work.

> LOVER #1: I don't love you any more!
> LOVER #2: I'm not the easiest person in the world to live with or love, am I.
> LOVER #1: (Pause.) You're damn right you're not . . .
> LOVER #2: Is this something you want to talk about, or is that that?

We'll grant you that Lover #2 is pretty good at keeping her cool, but she also knows that nobody makes a point of telling you he doesn't love you if that's all there is to it. So she moves up alongside him, giving him all the room to move around in that he needs.

> LOVER #1: I don't know . . .
> LOVER #2: It must have hurt you to have to tell me you don't love me any more.
> LOVER #1: I didn't want to say it . . .
> LOVER #2: You needed to.
> LOVER #1: (Long pause.) I don't know. It's just that I feel you're so distant sometimes. I want you to love me more and pay attention to me.
> LOVER #2: (Pauses and waits.)
> LOVER #1: I love you so much, sometimes it makes me crazy . . . I'm sorry I said it.

It's very important that Lover #2 "pauses and waits." She doesn't offer any excuses or defenses for alleged distantness. What is at stake is Lover #1's feelings and perceptions, not whether or not they are correct. The feelings are felt even if they don't conform to Lover #2's perception of reality. Remember, it's not the answer to life to have everybody who's wrong know that you are right. If the relationship is worth preserving, then what's to be gained by arguing over perceptions?

The second stage, the lead, actually begins when Lover #2 says, "You needed to." She redirects #1's focus back into what he needs, what lies underneath the attack. That is her estimation of the best way to help him restore his balance. Then, at his own pace, he comes up with the realization that he wanted only her attention, and not her absence.

The lead can continue:

> LOVER #2: Let's try to solve the problem. Let's see what kinds of real changes we can make so you get the attention you want and I still feel like my own person too.

They can now move along and find substantive solutions to the conflict. They can agree to be open with each other; they can agree to be more honest when they feel lonely or smothered; they can establish special times when no other interruptions are tolerated—in short, they have as many options as their joint and confluent creative energies allow them.

Now, to forestall your complaint that life is not as smooth as what we just showed you, bear in mind two things: First, *it can be* if you let it, and second, you must be able to use other responses if they are called for. Let's imagine that Lover #1 was no way near being available to confluence.

Let's say that all of #2's attempts to side with him were for nought. No matter what she says, he just keeps charging ahead.

> LOVER #1: You're damn right you're not easy to live with. You're distant, you're arrogant, you're insensitive, and you don't give a good goddamn about me!
>
> LOVER #2: What do you want to do about it?
>
> LOVER #1: I just told you! I don't love you any more!
>
> LOVER #2: (Waits and waits. She shifts into a square mode and does nothing. She must let him fall off balance by himself before she can restore it.)
>
> LOVER #1: Well? Why don't you say something?
>
> LOVER #2: I love you and I'm sorry you feel this way. I'm sorry you feel so much pain.

Notice how easily Lover #2 is able to shift from round (Aiki) to square (Doing Nothing) and back to round because she holds her own balance and refuses to let herself become trapped. It's almost as if most attackers are diseased: You can catch the disease, or you can stay healthy and help them to where *you* are. We'll grant you that inside Lover #2 may have been screaming with fear: fear of rejection, of humiliation, of loneliness, of all manner of terrible futures. But she held her balance (even after a momentary shock) and "won" because she didn't let her fear take over. If fear drives the machinery, you end up with a battlefield full of corpses. Sure, if Lover #1 keeps up his diseased behavior, it's possible that Lover #2 may well fall out of love herself. But at this point in the conflict she wanted to hold on to him, so she gave him the freedom to grow up.

How about the secretary who tells her boss, "I don't blame you," when he says he doesn't like her work? Her approach to confluence adds the element of surprise. He stares at her with a question mark all over his face. She is right: It isn't up to her to blame him for not liking her work. She isn't admitting that her work is terrible; she is taking that first step to get next to him. Her job, as she sees it, is to lead him to be more specific so that they can work out a mutually acceptable solution to the difficulty which the boss has decided to perceive.

> BOSS: You don't *blame* me?
> SECRETARY: It's not up to me to blame anybody for feeling the way they do. You're not happy, and I can't quibble with that.
> BOSS: (Puzzled.) But you think your work is up to par?
> SECRETARY: It can't be if you're not happy with it. My job is to be your secretary; that's what you hired me for.
> BOSS: I don't understand.

The boss has now lost his balance completely. He's made an attack, but his secretary is now over on his side of the line, helping him. She's not taking anything personally, but she's managed to objectify the conflict and help him see it a bit clearer too. That's what is confusing him.

> SECRETARY: If you don't think I should be fired outright, let's see if we can't work together on this thing and make it mutually acceptable. Like, what are some of your complaints?

She has the lead, and she's helping him deal as an adult instead of an arrogant bully fresh from the jungle gym.

BOSS: Well, uh, it's your letters. They don't look right.

SECRETARY: Every secretarial school preaches its own format. Give me an example of which one you prefer and I'll follow it. What else?

BOSS: I, uh, guess, I uh, overreacted a little bit. I'm sorry. I've had this commission thing over my head for the last six weeks, and I've been behaving like Attila the Hun. I'm sorry. And your letters look fine.

SECRETARY: Life's tough, isn't it, Mr. Forbes.

BOSS: (Smiling.) Yeah, and I guess I've been making it tougher.

Harmony. And she has given a gift to Mr. Forbes. She's helped him regain his equilibrium and see things in better perspective. And she's accomplished this by *not* clinging precariously to her image of herself as a good secretary or good person. Look how much she gained by risking the whole damn image.

Sure, it's hard to use Aiki at first, and, ironically, it'll take more inventiveness than all your flight-or-fight habits combined. But the bottom line, the final result of your efforts, will be worth every bit of it. Provided you bear in mind the following:

1) Aiki is composed of two basic actions: confluence—joining with the attack to empathize with the attacker and get out of his way—and lead—bringing the attacker back to balance.

2) Aiki can be used to deal with any attack at any time and any place. It's your option, dictated by all the elements you've already learned. Sure, there are times when it is less appropriate: A child who's ready to toss a brick through your plate-glass picture window needs to be stopped before you can even begin to empathize with him. And if there is a

life-or-death situation, we recommend that you save the lives (yours and others) first, using the most immediate strategy you can. Your first responsibility is to the living principle.

3) Every attacker has a right to his feelings; they may be based on an "incorrect" deduction from the facts, but the attacker is still feeling them. You cannot lead him to a "correct" perception without first becoming confluent with the perception *he* is experiencing.

In short, Attack-tics *demands* that you respect your attacker's rights and privileges while still protecting your own.

Thus far we've covered, if only briefly, all six types of defense against attacks. We've pointed out that Aiki is the most flexible and the most effective in most situations.

But we've been dealing so far with direct attacks: Somebody comes up to you and tells you off. Your boss reads you the riot act. Your wife yells at you. Your child gives you some lip. Those attacks come at you across a short line— from the attacker direct to you. But what about sneak attacks? What about disguised, dishonest attacks? Gossip? Rumor? How do you deal with somebody who stabs you in the back?

In the next chapter we'll tell you how.

VII

Aiki and
the Circular Attack

What people say behind your back
is your standing in the community.

—E.W. Howe
Country Town Sayings

In martial arts or even street terms, a circular attack is one
you can't see coming. The attacker comes at you from behind
or from your "blind" side. Taken off the street and into the
boardroom and bedroom, the circular attack is one which is
designed to deceive or confuse its target. It can also buy time
for the attacker.

Let's examine these one by one.

Circular attacks designed to deceive. Wolves traditionally
made their attacks on herds of buffalo by circling around the
shaggy foodstuffs and coming up from the downwind side.
The buffalo were thereby deceived by their own sense of
smell into thinking that the area was safe from predators.

Though their teeth are not always as sharp as those of the
wolf, gossips employ the same sort of circular attack. They

smile the smiles of friendship as they walk in front of us, then move around behind us and tell X or Y or Z that we are the worst human beings on the face of the earth. Mrs. Brown hugs Hazel and five minutes later is telling Mrs. Gray and Mrs. Black that Hazel is a liar and a thief. Hazel stands by, as unsuspecting as a buffalo, until she is ultimately felled by Mrs. Brown's circular attack.

Circular attacks designed to confuse. To keep our Western motif alive, just imagine the Indian attacks on pioneer wagon trains. The relentless Indians found early on that by riding around and around in circles they could befuddle and cloud the defenders' minds until they were able to grasp the complete advantage and make a direct attack. The pioneers, who were used to direct frontal assaults on fortified positions, found that nothing in their experience could help them respond effectively to the rings of attacking red men.

Every day sneaky folks employ much the same kind of tactic on us. There are those who seem to be all over us, giving us all sorts of conflicting signals at the same time. Mr. Rome invites Mr. Troy to his home and on the way, with a perpetual smile, makes veiled references to people like Mr. Troy who have failed in one way or another. Over dinner Mr. Rome uses expressions like "I don't want to nitpick but . . ." and "It's none of my business but . . .", continuing his disguised assault on Mr. Troy from every conceivable angle. Every time Mr. Troy tries to explore in words what's going on, Mr. Rome disavows any knowledge of his desire to hurt Mr. Troy's feelings. He counters by saying, "Don't you think you're getting awfully sensitive, Troy, old man?" By the time Troy leaves, he's a wreck, a wagon train burned to the ground.

Circular attacks designed to buy time. In essence, all circular attacks give the attacker the advantage of extra time. Since he engineers the attack in secret, he can keep sending confusing or deceptive signals until he feels the moment is right to go for the throat. The victim is forced to wait until some third party comes in and reveals all: "You should hear what your cousin is saying about you behind your back." Until that point he has been ignorant of the fact that his cousin has been chipping away at his base of support, hoping that when things *do* become known all the injured party's defenses won't be worth a newspaper in a windstorm.

Is all this designed to make you paranoid? Should you shun your friends in case they're planning to do you in? Nope. Remember that spot on your torso two inches below your navel? Your center? You can use this unique "organ" to keep you from being devastated or, oddly enough, surprised.

The center is a sensory organ of a sort. We don't know how it operates, but it does—if you let it. You'll find that if you stay centered at all times, your center will pick up messages, "vibes" from the people around you. The point is, you must pay attention. At first you'll just sense a kind of uneasiness in the pit of your stomach. You might even question your own perception. Later you'll learn to trust the messages your center sends you and to recognize them for what they are: hints that all is not right where you are or with whom you are dealing. *Trust the messages; stay centered.*

HOW TO HANDLE THE CIRCULAR ATTACK

An attack is an attack is an attack is an attack—no matter whether it comes with a kitchen knife or a smile. Each of the principles of Attack-tics you've learned so far is valid in some way in any attack situation. It's just that some attacks come right at you like a locomotive down a track, while others are roundabout.

To respond to a circular attack, you move straight on a line and then join into the circle. Your job is to become circular in order to help your attacker regain his balance.

To represent this kind of an attack, we begin with a circular arrow to represent the attacker and a square to represent you. In figure 1 below, you are standing still, waiting for the timing to be right. Let's see what takes place as you respond to the attack.

What exactly is happening? Let's let the arrow point represent the point of the attack. The last place you want to be is standing out there waiting for it to pierce you from the side or behind. So, paradoxically, *the safest place to be is inside, right next to the person who's doing the dishonest attacking.* The safest place to deal with a roundhouse punch is right next to the puncher, out of the way of the fist that's circling around in the air.

Most of the time you also have the option of Withdrawing from any of these circular attacks, but for now let's examine a situation in which a resolution is required. Let's say that Gail and Sandy work in the same office and must keep on working together. Someone tells Gail that Sandy is bad-mouthing her behind her back. Since Gail can't simply remove herself from the conflict, her goal is to force Sandy to make her attack directly and stop all this backstabbing. And there's no doubt in anybody's mind that backstabbing and gossiping are truly circular attacks on Gail. At first, as in figure 1 of our diagram, Gail is standing squarely, choosing to Do Nothing, finding her center and holding on to her balance. When the attack is brought to her attention, she shifts into the triangular mode and, with clear intention, moves in close to Sandy, following the point of her triangle (figure 2). Gail is safer standing right next to Sandy. For one

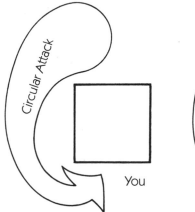

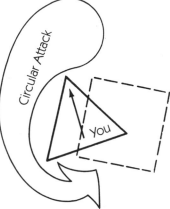

Figure 1

Figure 2

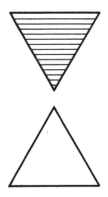

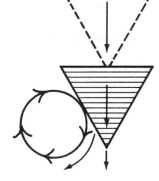

Figure 3

Figure 4

thing, Sandy can't keep badmouthing her behind her back, because there *is* no back, only front. And as soon as Sandy is forced to make a direct attack, Gail can shift into the circular mode and use Aiki.

It's not as difficult as it sounds. Let's play out the drama to see how it's done.

Gail has heard from a third party that behind her back Sandy has been spreading the rumor that she sleeps around with anybody who might advance her career.

This happens not to be true: Gail is not promiscuous. She's very attractive and very alive; she's the kind of person many men are easily drawn to. Evidently Sandy, out of her own neurotic needs, is quite actively trying to injure Gail. But whether or not Gail sleeps around is not the issue. Gail has the God-given right to behave any way she sees fit, provided that she doesn't hurt anyone in the process. Sandy, on the other hand, does not have the right to injure Gail or Gail's reputation for any reason whatsoever.

When the word drifts down to Gail, she is furious. She's also saddened by the realization that people can be so cruel to one another. And she feels betrayed, because she has always thought that she and Sandy "got along okay." If not close friends, they do speak often and sometimes they have lunch together.

So Gail has temporarily lost her center. Energy is flowing through her, her mind flicks into high gear, and she begins to imagine all kinds of gory revenge. She's especially fond of Plan A, in which she thoroughly humiliates Sandy in front of her co-workers. A great plan, right?

Wrong.

It would be foolish to expose Sandy in front of friends and allies who could rush to her defense. If Gail's counterattack is as successful as she hopes it will be, the onlookers might be tempted to see Sandy as the poor pathetic victim of nasty Gail's plotting. More important, however, Gail is looking for resolution, not the destruction of a human being. She has learned an important Attack-tics principle: *Destroyed people make bad enemies.*

The very first step in using Attack-tics, before you begin *any* course of action, is to center.

Gail regains her center. She concentrates on her one-spot, relaxes, throws away all the nagging self-doubt ("Gee, what am I doing that would give people cause to gossip?") and anger ("What a rotten friend Sandy is!"), and begins to examine her options, one by one. By virtue of the fact that the attack is distant and circular, she has one important advantage: the time to go home and figure out a course of action. She knows that the situation must be dealt with, but she also knows that there is no immediacy; one more night of bad-mouthing is not going to change things drastically. (It's interesting to note that the attacker's original time advantage becomes the victim's advantage once she becomes conscious of the attack.)

So Gail goes home to carefully plan her resolution to the problem. Her first step is to select a time and place that will maximize her efforts. A lunch hour would be too short, so she decides to ask Sandy to stop by for a drink after work. Sandy, curious about Gail's apartment, accepts the invitation.

Several times along the way Gail has to remind herself that this is not a military operation. She keeps hold of her center, remembering that she is acting out of the protective spirit: She's protecting herself from future attack and she's protecting Sandy from the disease that seems to be consuming her. In short, she is moving closer to Sandy's center all the time. Meanwhile, Sandy is thinking to herself that she'll have some good stuff tomorrow, after she's seen "where the damage is done . . ."

They arrive at Gail's apartment. After some preliminary conversation, Gail goes straight in in the triangular mode, like a falcon on a weasel. (See figure 2.)

> GAIL: Sandy, you've been telling people that I'm sleeping with every man in the office!
> SANDY: I have not! Who's been telling you that?
> GAIL: For the last three months you've told a dozen different people that I sleep with anyone who'll raise my salary.
> SANDY: Who said that? They're lying to you!
> GAIL: I want you to stop wrecking my reputation. I've never done anything to you.
> SANDY: What do you mean, you've never done anything to me!

Notice that Gail never leaves her line of intention to debate whether or not Sandy's charges are true. She doesn't allow herself to be diverted. She keeps herself in the triangular mode, trying to get Sandy to stop circling her. By saying "I've never done anything to you," Gail is opening the possibility for Sandy's counterattack.

Gail is successful. When Sandy next speaks, it is as a triangle with a straightforward, *honest* attack. (See figure 3.)

> SANDY: What do you mean, you've never done anything to me! What about Nelson? You knew I was seeing him, but you went behind my back and did your fluttery-eyelids number on him! You're out to steal everybody's man, and you won't be satisfied till you've had them all!

As in the case of Robin Hood and Little John, the conflict is now out front on the log. It is no longer circular. Gail can now use any of the six options—or a combination. She realizes that this is not a win/lose event: She doesn't need to defeat Sandy, but she must get her to cease and desist gossiping. Besides, she knows from Sandy's actions that the girl already feels like a loser; it would not be in the protective spirit to make her more of a loser. For these reasons alone, Gail chooses Aiki. (See figure 4.)

GAIL: I wish I'd known how you felt before this. I can understand what you're going through. It hurts.

SANDY: You're damn right it hurts!

GAIL: So now you want to hurt me. I don't blame you!

SANDY: If it hadn't been for you, Nelson and I would still be together!

GAIL: I can see where you would think that.

SANDY: (Pause.) What does that mean?

GAIL: Well, you never came to me to ask me what was going on. It's tough to sit around. Your imagination starts telling you all kinds of things. I've been there, and I know what you must have felt.

SANDY: I don't understand.

GAIL: I never went out with Nelson. Who told you I did?

SANDY: *He* did!

GAIL: He doesn't like rejection. He asked me a few times, and I turned him down. I knew you two were dating.

SANDY: I don't believe you.

GAIL: I wouldn't either if I were you.

SANDY: (Long pause.) You really didn't go out with him?

GAIL: No.

SANDY: That liar!

GAIL: Nelson's like everybody else. He's got problems. He's in pain too.

SANDY: (Crying.) Oh, Gail, I'm sorry . . .

GAIL: Thank you, Sandy. Nothing's as easy as people say it is, is it.

SANDY: No . . . What can I do about Nelson?

GAIL: What would you like to do?

SANDY: Make him love me again.

GAIL: Do what you have to, then.

Compare the way things worked out in this actual scene with the image Gail had in her head when she lost her center: the one where Sandy stood in front of her friends, the object of scorn and ridicule. What would that vendetta have accomplished? Would Gail have gone home feeling wonderful? If so, the satisfaction would have been short-lived, and she would have made an implacable enemy. We're going to suggest that that kind of victory—the kind that causes someone else's defeat—feels good for a few moments or even a few hours, but ultimately the cost is much too great.

Instead, what we got was a whole Sandy, who will not only quit attacking Gail but will be reunited with her own spirit and the rest of the human race. You may quibble with her desire to get back with the rather untrustworthy Nelson, but her fight with Gail is over. Gail can now go to sleep as a balanced person who knows she can deal effectively with most of what life has to offer.

Briefly, what happened? Gail moved in on a direct line and confronted Sandy with the problem. She forced Sandy to attack and then chose Aiki as a response to that attack. She moved from square to triangular to round and "won" by "giving in." It's almost that simple.

A SPECIAL CASE

Sometimes that triangular move in can be a bit less direct while still preserving the triangular spirit. With a bit of Deception you can achieve the same result.

Let's say that you are up against somebody who will *never* confess to backstabbing. You know that no matter how much you say "You've been stabbing me in the back," his

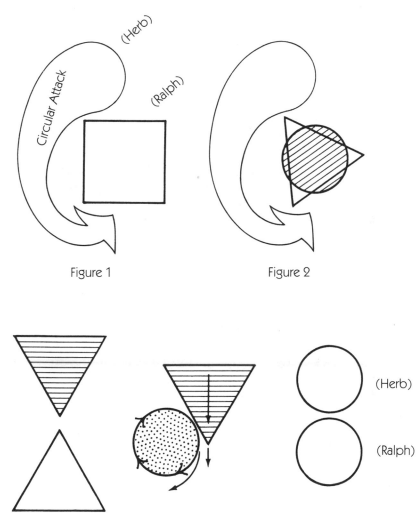

Figure 1

Figure 2

Figure 3

Figure 4

Figure 5

response will be "I don't know where you've gotten your information, but it's patently false." Sad to say, there are thousands of these folks who would rather die on their feet than admit to being dishonest, sneaky people. Their smiles are twice as indelible, and you must work harder to provoke their direct attack.

Herb and Ralph are teachers at a junior high school. There's always been tension between them, at least so far as Ralph is concerned. Ralph is a free-wheeling spirit who teaches in a relaxed, "modern" way, and Herb is a much more traditional kind of pedagogue. Herb conceals his dislike of Ralph, except when he gets one or two other faculty members alone. On these occasions he makes fun of Ralph's experimental learning methods and satirizes the younger man's whole approach to life. It wouldn't bother Ralph much except for the fact that Herb's criticisms may prejudice administrators against him and directly affect his freedom to teach the best way he knows how. Thus, when he learns of Herb's tactics (figure 1), he knows he must deal with them directly.

Ralph realizes that Herb is so far gone, so devious and, paradoxically, so smilingly polite, that he'll never admit to what he's been doing and saying. So, in a sense, Ralph must trick Herb into making a frontal attack. As soon as the frontal attack is made, Ralph can then make his choice of response.

Selecting his time and place carefully, Ralph walks into Herb's classroom at the end of the day.

> RALPH: Herb, I've got a bone to pick with you.
> HERB: I beg your pardon?
> RALPH: I'm really quite angry about the grading curve you've been using on the seventh-graders!

In truth, Ralph couldn't care less about Herb's grading curve. His object is to coax Herb into a counterattack. So he picks on Herb's pride and joy, his bell curve. (See figure 2.) Herb is caught so off guard that he begins to rant and rave (figure 3).

HERB: You don't like my grading curve? Well, let me tell you one thing, you little upstart, if your attitude to teaching was one sixth as serious as mine, if your way of handling your students was one sixth as appropriate, you might just *begin* to be a good teacher.

RALPH: I didn't know you felt that way about my work with the students.

HERB: You're damn right I feel that way. It's teachers like you who're making the students so disruptive in school. Giving them too much freedom.

RALPH: I feel the same way you do.

HERB: (Pause.) What?

RALPH: I'd like to sit down with you and talk about what we can both do about the problem of disruptive students. At the same time, it might give me a chance to explain what I've been doing with them. I know we both want to solve the problem. [See figure 4.]

The outcome of that event was Herb stopped his backstabbing and both men came to understand and appreciate (if not agree with) the other's position. (See figure 5.) At no time did Herb apologize for his previous behavior, but this was not Ralph's objective. All he wanted was to get the backstabbing stopped, not to make the older man grovel in remorseful apology. Nor did Ralph play the shrink and point out that perhaps Herb was feeling threatened by Ralph's energy and his popularity with the kids. Ralph stuck with the problem, using Aiki to flow with the older man's anxieties about what the school was coming to. He could have employed other options, but he knew that his chances of reaching some degree of harmony with Herb would be best if he began with

Aiki confluence. To get there, however, it was necessary to feign an attack in an entirely different direction.

It is important to bear in mind that in both of these dramas, neither Ralph nor Gail lost anything—unless you consider the loss of revenge a loss. We don't!

To sum up, in dealing with the circular attack your first job is to get the attacker to deal with you on a straight line, to be honest, to reveal himself, to give up his or her round-about aggression and face the conflict which lies underneath. To do this, *you must move in close and find a way to provoke a direct attack.* Always move from your center, in a balanced, protective way. The centering helps in keeping you from being afraid of confrontation while restraining your less productive urge for revenge. As soon as the circular attacker begins to attack forthrightly, and not until then, you are in a position (again from your center) to select any appropriate conflict response. While we have repeatedly stressed the use of the Aiki option, the other five are always open to you.

Frankly, circular attacks are the most difficult type to handle, because half the time we can't see them, and the other half we'd rather not see them. You may hear that somebody is talking about you behind your back, and want to do something about it, but you're afraid to. You are afraid to confront your "hidden" aggressor even though you know that the only real resolution will come about through confrontation. What you forget is that sneaky aggressors are just as afraid of confrontation—if they weren't, they'd come right at you on a straight line and tell you off to your face! So you can use that knowledge and, instead of dwelling on your own fears, move forward with confidence in an effort to help your attacker confront *his* or *her* fears.

At the very least, remember that circular attacks won't stop unless *you* stop them.

VIII

A Day in the Life

Boast not thyself of tomorrow;
for thou knowest not what a
day may bring forth.

—Proverbs 27:I

To paraphrase the poet, by the time the next thousand years rolls around, we'll have forgotten all about our present troubles. But for now we go through whole days in which the highs are very high and the lows are very low. We read our sun signs in the newspapers to see if tomorrow will bring joy or sadness. And although we know that the slips in fortune cookies were printed in New Jersey, we hope the one that says "Success is just around the corner" was really really meant for us and nobody else. Chief among our daily pains are the conflicts—troops and troops of them—which pop up in front of us like targets at a shooting range.

It doesn't have to be that way.

Now that we've been through the basics of Attack-tics, let's see how we might make use of them. Armed with our new skills, we'll face a day in the life, your life, and see what happens when you keep your center, approach conflict as a given in nature, and deal with it from a protective spirit. The specific details may not fit your personal lifestyle, job, etc., but bear in mind that conflict is conflict whether it be engaged in by a mother and a four-year-old, a boss and an employee, a teacher and a student, or a husband and a wife. You should be able to make the parallels to your own situation.

6:45 A.M.

Your alarm was set for seven, but at a quarter to seven you get a phone call. A wrong number. The world's foremost practical joker once said anyone dumb enough to dial a wrong number deserves whatever you give him. But you resist the temptation to tell the man asking for Harry that Harry died last night and simply say, "You've got the wrong number." You don't fight back, though you could; instead, you Do Nothing. Your time is too important for you to get into a shouting match with somebody too sleepy to dial correctly. You pat yourself on the back and congratulate yourself for regaining your center so early in the day. Wrong numbers aren't win/lose contests anyway, so you go with the flow and take the extra fifteen minutes in the shower as a reward.

7:35 A.M.

You have four minutes in which to get downstairs and into your car in order to make work on time. It's your schedule, and it works very well for you. *But* your mother calls just as you're going out the door, and begins talking before you can explain the situation.

MOM: I hope it's not true what I heard about you.

Certainly, that opening line is enough to pique anybody's curiosity, if not arouse their anger, but there just isn't time to continue the conversation, and you know from past experience that your mother just loves to attack in this dishonest way. Since this is a no-win situation, and because you decide that work takes priority over an early-morning squabble, you choose Deception as your response.

> YOU: Mom, I've got a doctor's appointment, and if I'm late he won't see me.
> MOM: Nothing serious?
> YOU: Just a checkup. Call you later.

With that taken care of, you're ready to go. Up only an hour, you've used Doing Nothing, on the wrong number, and Deception and Withdrawal, on your mother. The odds are that you've begun to feel pretty good about your competence to handle what the day will bring. You feel centered and strong.

7:48 A.M.

A car cuts you off at an intersection. You could get furious about it, but you remain on center, realizing that a fight will only delay you, that it might mess up your car, and, further, that life is too short for you to appoint yourself driving instructor to the masses. You choose to Do Nothing, and you're even happier because *they* aren't getting to you today.

8:30 A.M.

"Look what the cat dragged in" is the favorite opening conversational gambit of the office nurd. He's always saying things like "You look like yesterday's leftovers," "Jeez, with a face like yours you oughta stay home." In a sense, these are attacks and they are not attacks. They are his way of saying "Hello, I really hope you like me." As irritating as these statements are, you've decided that it's more fun to flow with them than to wheel around on him and get into a verbal battle. Instead, you've made it a game for yourself to find a different Aiki response to each of his carpings. You're in no position to heal his bent personality, but you can help him by flowing with what's underneath his attacks.

> NURD: Look what the cat dragged in.
> YOU: I'm glad you care. I mean, I really had another rough night.
> NURD: The opposite sex really goes for a face like yours?
> YOU: I don't understand it either.

And off you go to your battle station, leaving the nurd feeling that you do care, that perhaps he can risk being a little more straightforward with you next time.

9:15 A.M.

The boss strides into your office waving a sheaf of papers and says, "Why the hell did you do it *this* way!"

It doesn't really matter what the "it" refers to. Every minute of every day some boss is walking into someone's office and saying something like that, whether the "it" is machine fittings, audit reports, shoe sizes, or ledgers. Most employees do one of two things: They shrivel up or they get huffy, with statements such as "I did it that way because *you* told me to—if you'll remember . . ." But that's not the way you're going to respond—not *this* time!

You know that you're standing right in the middle of a frontal attack; you don't need a hostility meter to tell you that much. The boss, waving the papers in your face, looks one step away from a myocardial infarction: purple veins, a throbbing artery running up and down his neck, absolutely tortured breathing. The last thing you want is to be his victim. So you recenter yourself. You breathe out slowly.

Point one goes through your mind: *This is not a contest.* If it were, you could step up to the plate, knock one out of the park, and retire happily as the winning batter. However, if you hit a homer over the boss's head you will probably have only your batting average to keep you warm during the next energy crisis. Besides, it should be obvious to you that he needs help.

You then ask yourself: *Is this the time or place for dealing with this conflict?* You may have no choice, but it's still worth making sure that you really *do* have no choice. You decide that you must respond immediately and right where you are.

Actually, you have already begun to respond: You have begun by Doing Nothing. You haven't gone to sleep; you've been an active listener. Settled into the square mode, you've been counting on your balance and stability to keep you from being blown away by the force of the boss's attack. You've been actively watching for clues and signs so that you would be able to make the appropriate response. Moreover, Doing Nothing allows you to change your mind three or four times before you commit yourself, especially since this is your boss you're dealing with.

Finally, you've made your choice. The solution, you decide, the *harmony,* probably lies in Parley—a compromise.

The big problem will be to get your boss to yield his triangular attack mode and become circular so that Parley is possible. As he rants on about the poor quality of your work, you enter in.

    YOU: May I have a look?

Already your calm behavior is modeling an appropriate response to the situation. What you want is to get the boss to focus on the problem at hand. You take your time. Then:

    YOU: What do you see as the major difficulty with what's here?
    BOSS: It isn't clear, and nobody could understand it.
    YOU: Which parts don't you understand?
    BOSS: *All* of it!
    YOU: Since we're both in this together, let's see if we can't unravel it. I don't want to send out anything that's unclear, but I'll need your specific help to clean it up. What about the first paragraph?
    BOSS: Do you mean that we *are* ready to bargain with the Greenfeld Company or we *aren't*?
    YOU: Okay, I mean we *are* ready, but I guess I can see where that sentence could be misconstrued.

You are now fully into the Parley mode. You won't have to rewrite every word, and if the boss responds to your harmonious approach, you'll end up with a better end product—which, as we keep repeating, is far more important than seeing your opponent defeated, and ending up with an ego which depends on destruction for its growth.

Eventually the boss leaves your office—with an apology for having been so irate. You're pleased that you've come up with a better letter (or memo or whatever it was he was so upset about).

11:20 A.M.

You get a phone call from your lover.

You're already centered, because you've made it a practice never to answer the telephone without first reminding yourself to regain your center. In the old days you were always caught off guard by telephone calls; now you're always relaxed and alert.

Your love interest starts out the conversation normally enough, but soon gets into a heavy subject: He or she feels hemmed in and wants the freedom to date other people. Instead of letting your feelings of rejection take over, you redouble your efforts to stay on balance. The attack is too serious to be dealt with in your old way. The first challenge is to recognize that this *is* an attack: Nobody calls the person they're in love with to tell them they'll be seeing other lovers without at least a subconscious desire to inflict pain—no matter how many times the word "honesty" is used. The difficulty is to stay objective enough to handle the situation.

Once again you consider the time and place.

Obviously, they are both wrong. Your lover has you at a complete disadvantage. You can't see his or her face or body, so you can't properly judge the spirit or assess your conflict response. You are sure of only one thing: You can't continue in the relationship with the terms that are being offered you.

Instead of arguing the point over the phone, you Withdraw, reserving your other options for later.

> YOU: Listen, I can't handle this right now. You've got me at a complete disadvantage. I want to work this out with you, because I care very much what happens. Let's meet after work and talk about it.
> LOVER: I've said everything I want to say.

> YOU: Then it'll be a chance to say how I feel.
> LOVER: It won't make any difference.
> YOU: Do I deserve a chance to try?
> LOVER: Okay. See you at five thirty at Barney's.

What has just happened is that you had to become triangular in order to Withdraw and set up an alternative time and place, and still your lover ended up choosing the time and place: immediately after work, at a bar that is usually crowded and noisy. Wrong for you. Sure, you could retaliate further, saying you don't like Barney's, etc., but you can do better than that. You shift into the Deceptive mode.

> YOU: I won't be free by five thirty. Let me take you to dinner. I'll pick you up at seven.
> LOVER: (Pause.) Okay . . .

Withdrawal is not always easy, but how much could you have accomplished over the phone, and in an office where you have other responsibilities? In addition, you've given both of you time to think—a definite plus in an emotionally charged situation.

Now your job is twofold: to keep from spending all day fantasizing about the impending confrontation, and to prepare for it well.

The second is a lot easier than the first. In order to prepare for it, all you need is to figure out your priorities. Take some quiet time for yourself, and establish just how much the relationship means to you. Ask yourself some specific questions, and answer them without letting your ego run away with the game. Explore what might be behind your lover's attack. Is the desire to date other people a sincere need? a threat to get you firmly tied down? a piece of misplaced anger about some other problem? What is your lover's history in this regard? What was your last conflict about? There are no right or wrong answers here; the process should help you respond in the way best for you both.

Resisting the urge to fantasize is more difficult. Withdrawal allows us the time to solve problems quietly, but it also gives us time to roil about in anxieties, self-doubts, and conjectures. "Concentration" is the key word here: Concentrate on your center and on your breathing. Each time fantasy or doubt shoves its way into your consciousness or seduces your mind away from the problem at hand, recenter, breathe out, and calm yourself until you can move forward again.

12:45 P.M.

You use lunchtime to consider the conflict with your lover. You decide that when you meet later you're going to take the initiative. You're still reserving your other options, but you sense that his or her attack was not straightforward, that it was an attempt to sound the depths of your affection. You also conclude that he or she is well worth fighting for.

1:35 P.M.

You come back from lunch and remember that you must return your mother's call. You completely forgot! Reminding yourself to keep on balance, you dial her number.

> YOU: Hi, Mom, what was your problem this morning?
> MOM: How was your checkup?
> YOU: I'm perfect in every way.
> MOM: I'm glad.

YOU: What were you going to tell me this morning?

MOM: It was nothing.

YOU: Okay. How's everything else?

MOM: It really *was* something.

YOU: Shoot.

MOM: I don't know how to say it.

YOU: I can take it.

MOM: Your sister says you're sleeping around. I thought we taught you better than that.

YOU: Why do you suppose she said that?

MOM: I don't know. Maybe she thought I could do something about it . . .

YOU: How did you feel when she told you?

MOM: Terrible. I cried.

YOU: Since she didn't tell *me*, I didn't feel a thing. Did she tell you what "sleeping around" means?

MOM: *You* know what it means.

YOU: Is five lovers sleeping around? One? A dozen?

MOM: One is more than enough.

YOU: What would you like to hear me say?

MOM: That you're *not* sleeping around.

YOU: Why is this upsetting you so much, Mom?

MOM: I don't know. I know you're an adult, but it's hard to remember. I don't want you tossing your life away.

YOU: Do you know why you believed my sister?

MOM: Why would she lie?

YOU: I don't think she lied. I think she's unhappy, and I think she doesn't know me very well. I think she loves you very much and wants to look good in your eyes. I'm not sleeping around. I'm sorry she bothered you, and I wish she'd bothered me instead.

MOM: I'm sorry.

YOU: Me too.

Good. You chose to Parley with your mother in a very protective manner. You didn't become defensive about your lifestyle, because it does not really concern her. You are an adult and don't need your parents to validate your life choices. Instead, you kept her focused on the *real* problem: your sister. You asked questions to help your mother reframe what had happened so that both of you could consider the event from a common point. Best of all, you waited to say that you were not sleeping around until the very end, because you knew that if you'd said it at the beginning your mother would have considered the Parley over. That's really all she wanted to hear, but you needed to have her hear the other points as well. Most people begin by defending themselves: "I'm not sleeping around . . ." They end up losing the audience they want to address.

Now it remains for you to confront your sister. You're angry that she said those things, and you're also angry that she would tattle to mother. You'll have to respond to her circular attack.

1:55 P.M.

You call her.

>   YOU: (In the triangular mode.) Why on earth did you feel
>   it necessary to tell Mom that I've been sleeping
>   around!
> SISTER: What! I never said that. You know Mom. I may have
>   said you seemed to be enjoying yourself on a lot of
>   dates, but I never said you were sleeping around! She
>   asked me how you were doing, and I told her.
>   YOU: Come on now.
> SISTER: (Pause.) Well, goddammit, you're acting like a fool

with all those dates. People are beginning to talk, and I don't want to be related to you if you're going to keep on that way!

YOU: (Shifting into Aiki confluence.) I can see where you're being embarrassed.

SISTER: That's not the half of it. I worry about you. I don't want you to end up on the junkpile.

YOU: Thank you. You really care about me, don't you.

SISTER: I'm sorry. I should've told you instead of going to Mother, but I was upset.

YOU: I'm sorry you were so upset, because it's not true. I've only dated one person in the last four months.

SISTER: But . . . but Trudy said . . .

YOU: Trudy? What does Trudy know about my sex life? Why don't we both take it up with her?

SISTER: No, this is one I'll do on my own. I should never have listened to her. Jesus, I'm sorry.

YOU: We've got too much going to mess up our relationship like this. If you get worried again, come see me or call me.

SISTER: I will.

YOU: Thanks for loving me that much . . .

You made the correct choice: You moved in on a direct line to provoke your sister into a straightforward attack; when that was accomplished, you shifted into the circular mode and helped her come back to her own center. She realized how off balance she'd been, and your relationship was strengthened instead of being destroyed.

2:05 P.M.

Around about this time you realize that one of your colleagues, a man you beat out for a promotion, has been avoiding you, and going silent whenever you're in his vicinity. The silent treatment is a form of circular attack, and you must decide whether you want to deal with it. As there isn't a great deal at stake with this man, you decide to wait him out, Doing Nothing until he chooses to become more direct.

2:55 P.M.

You start worrying about the confrontation with your lover tonight. You recenter and focus on your breathing so you can get back to your work.

3:30 P.M.

You sail into the office of one of your supervisors, really excited about a project you've developed, a plan you've been working on, something which you've created. You think it is brilliant. You describe it or show it, and your supervisor says, "Forget it. It's dumb. How could you ever believe it would work?"

An attack, but one which you waltzed into, the way a log moves into a buzzsaw. It's too late to turn back and realize that you lost your center the minute you sailed into his office. It's too late to realize that you'd forgotten about this particular supervisor's character structure, that he's threatened by new ideas.

But you think about it a moment and realize this isn't a win/lose situation. Your idea is not dead because one person hates it. You still have a chance. You regain your center.

You assess the supervisor's spirit. Is there a lot of energy behind his attack? Is the attack directed more at you than at the idea, or the other way around? What is the relationship that has existed between you before this? Your disappointment could be a function of the fact that heretofore you'd been received so well by him.

Then you ask yourself that all-important question: Is this the right time, or is there another time that will work more in my favor?

Reading him as well as you can, you decide to shift into the Parley mode. You'll go to the mat on this one if you must, but if you're going to fight, you first want to know as much as you can about the opposition. In the Parley, he might play most of his cards.

> YOU: Where do you see its biggest shortcoming?
> SUPERVISOR: Look, just forget about it. No amount of diddling is gonna make it work.
> YOU: Okay, but I need to know where I went wrong thinking it would.
> SUPERVISOR: They tried it before I got here. It didn't work then and it won't work now.
> YOU: Is there any data I could see?
> SUPERVISOR: How should I know?
> YOU: Can you meet me halfway? I still like the idea. I know it's not perfect, and I'd like you to give me a hand. Explain to me where I went wrong. I don't want to keep coming up with stuff that won't work, so give me some help, will you?
> SUPERVISOR: Okay, leave it with me and I'll get back to you on it.

Now he is Withdrawing. It may be a dodge—just to get rid of you—or he may actually give your work another look. It won't do you any good to press your luck, so you agree and go back to your office. You make a note to follow up tomorrow or the next day if you receive no word.

All through that contretemps you were appealing to your

supervisor's better self. At times he may have been cantankerous or rude or insensitive, or all three, but you kept holding up to him a goal which his *better* self would appreciate: Help me so we can all be more efficient. Help me so we can all do better. Help me so you can feel good about yourself. Certainly your idea may be turned down, but you've given it your best shot. You didn't let your ego rain bombs on your attacker, and you focused on the problem. Too many people equate asking for help with flying a white flag. The person who sincerely asks for help rarely loses a conflict.

Things limp along for the rest of the afternoon, and at 5:00 P.M. you pull yourself together and head for home.

5:06 P.M.

In the parking lot you notice that the silent colleague's car is parked right next to yours. He's heading toward it, and you decide you don't need any extra problems left over for tomorrow. You watch him get closer and see him see you. For a moment it looks as if he might veer away, but he knows he's been spotted.

YOU: What's the trouble, Fred?
FRED: What?
YOU: What are you angry about?
FRED: I'm not angry. Why should I be?
YOU: Okay, then, I'm angry.
FRED: Huh?
YOU: You snubbed me all day.

Your strategy is to try to force this circular attacker to come clean.

FRED: So what!

YOU: I value your friendship, and if I did something to make you mad, I'd like to find out what it is.

FRED: Shit, you didn't do anything. I'm angry because I didn't get the promotion and you did. I'm angry at myself. I'm sorry. I guess I don't like losing.

YOU: What did you lose?

FRED: The job!

YOU: And I won it?

FRED: Yeah.

YOU: It was your competition that helped me. I didn't beat you, and you didn't lose. We both helped each other get better at what we do.

FRED: Yeah, but it's still tough to take.

YOU: Show me the clause in our contract where it said anything'll ever be easy.

FRED: Yeah, you're right.

For many people it's tough to "win." They feel guilty and they feel responsible for another person's "defeat." But you kept your center and realized that it wasn't a win/lose situation, even though there was only one job opening. You focused on what was important: that competition is not engaged in for its own sake; it is what makes people become better at what they do. Fred may have lost the promotion in a sense, but you led him to realize that he wasn't a loser.

From triangle to circle . . .

6:10 P.M.

You stop off at the supermarket to pick up a few things —ten items in all. The store is crowded, and you're tired, and you're not the world's foremost counter-of-items-in-shopping-carts, so you go to the express lane—nine items only— and wait patiently to be checked out.

That's when the man behind you begins doing a whole heavy-breathing-and-sighing routine. At first you wonder if he's having some physical problem; then you realize he's beginning to mumble about your having ten items in your shopping cart. He's actually counted all of them over your shoulder, and has decided that you are at least a villain, if not a desecrator of the flag. So far, despite his groans and sighs, his attack is circular, directed behind you but not at you. You're vaguely embarrassed, even a little piqued, but you don't feel like leaving this line to wait at the end of another for one crummy box of Woofburgers. And yet something protective also tells you that there are enough crazies loose in the world to fill all the jails and institutions. People have been maimed for less than having one extra can of dog food.

Do you draw him out of his circular attack? Do you wait, Doing Nothing and hoping it'll all pass? Do you Withdraw to a saner aisle and one which, properly, you belong in? Do you whip around on him and Fight Back with all your strength? Do you try to Deceive him, explaining that you have a sick child at home? Do you Parley, compromising by letting him ahead of you with his eight boxes of frozen french fries? Or do you try some kind of confluence?

Your quick assessment tells you that your second option is best: Doing Nothing. You decide to let him ramble on. If he becomes too abusive or threatening, you can always shift modes, but right now you become a square. Your center keeps you from feeling abused, and yet it also allows you to understand how truly painful life must be for this person, to whom one item is such a tragedy.

You pay your $7.85, collect your groceries, and withdraw, having neither won nor lost.

6:56 P.M.

You're outside your lover's front door. You're centering, checking your breathing. You know it's the only way to handle the anxieties about rejection which want to take you over. It's the only way to keep tonight from turning into a win/lose situation. Centering will be the key ingredient in your attack. It will keep you from letting the child inside you scream in pain. It will keep you from fighting dirty.

As you move into your lover's apartment you find that you're moving from your center. You're not sulking in or shuffling in, playing the poor little child whose feelings have been hurt. But you don't look like a hit man from New Jersey, either. You're walking in alert and relaxed, looking for the line which will connect you to your lover.

As the initial chitchat passes you by, you're concentrating on spirit: your lover's spirit. You're checking the facial expression, posture, and so forth. You're also open to the "messages" which your center is bringing you—those indefinable inklings and vague sensations which are being transmitted to you. You don't want to decide to Fight Back only to find that meanwhile your lover has changed his or her mind and become as soft as taffy.

But nothing has changed. You become a triangle.

> YOU: Listen to me. I don't want to date other people, I want to be with you. I have no feelings for other people. I care about you. I love you, but I can't accept your going out with other people.
> LOVER: I feel hemmed in, constricted.
> YOU: By what?
> LOVER: You.

YOU: Do you love me?
LOVER: Yes.
YOU: And I'm still constricting you?
LOVER: I feel constricted.

Things are not going badly for you at this point. Your lover has conceded that he or she still loves you and that the constriction might be coming from some other source. That source, you suspect, is inside your lover, but you'll have to help him or her uncover it, not bludgeon him or her with it.

YOU: Help me understand how you feel hemmed in.

You have shifted into Aiki confluence. You're now moving toward harmony, toward empathy, getting closer to the root of the problem.

LOVER: I don't feel I have any options.
YOU: I know the feeling. What would you like to do?
LOVER: Get out more. Do more.
YOU: Anything in particular?
LOVER: Travel. Go somewhere.
YOU: Where do you see yourself going?
LOVER: I don't know. Mexico . . . the Virgin Islands, maybe.

Now your problem is to resist the impulse to plug yourself into your lover's fantasies and say, "Well, I'll take you to Mexico." This would solve the immediate problem but not the larger difficulty.

YOU: That sounds like a good idea. Would it solve things for you if you took a week's vacation in Acapulco?
LOVER: (Pause.) I don't know. I guess not. I don't know what I want.
YOU: It's easier for me. I know what I want. I want

you. It must be much harder on you because of that.

LOVER: You seem so sure . . .

YOU: It's not anything I can make happen. I don't *try* to love you. Look, I don't want to constrict you. I'll leave you alone for as long as I can stand it. I'd rather you didn't date other people, but I can't force you not to. If you feel less constricted that way, less hemmed in, then that's what you want. If not, I'll be right here.

LOVER: I don't think that's what I want.

YOU: I know it's not what I want. But you owe it to yourself to give it a try.

LOVER: I don't want . . . I love you. I don't want you to go away, and I don't care if we never go to Mexico. I want you to be with me . . . all the time.

YOU: I'd like that.

So the scene between you and your lover is resolved by a sensitive shift of modes from Fighting Back to Parley to Aiki. You began by Fighting Back because you wanted to establish a firm base, make your intentions clear, and, in a sense, "shock" your partner's balance. You didn't know it at the time, but that fight response gave your lover the "proof" he or she needed of your affection. You risked a lot with your use of Aiki. If your lover had really wanted all that freedom, you might have found yourself separated for a month, or out in the cold altogether. But your taking the lead and offering to step back forced your lover to deal with the reality of a breakup. That reality was simply too much.

What happened is probably more typical than unusual. When you start using Aiki you begin to learn that often people's stated needs or desires are exactly the opposite of what they really want. Often the mother who asks her children to leave her alone wants their attention. Often the worker who talks about quitting wants more work, more recognition. But if you argue with someone's stated feelings, telling them they really don't want to do what they say they want to do, nine times out of ten they'll go ahead and do it. If you use Aiki instead, letting them reach their own conclusions, then the real underlying need will eventually surface. They will turn right around and admit they want the children or they want you or they want whatever. We'll bet that hundreds of thousands of "wrong" choices are made every day because people feel pushed into them by the opposition of friends and colleagues and lovers.

It's been a day! A day in the life. Viewed this way, with all the daily conflicts highlighted, your life appears to be like a soap-opera episode. We had to highlight the instances of conflict in order to demonstrate how Attack-tics can work, but now let's look at the very positive side of your last twenty-four hours.

First of all, and most important to you, you go to sleep with an incredible sense of wholeness born of your ability to enter into conflict and exit from it in a harmonious manner. You aren't tossing under a blanket of guilt engendered by a day full of overkill. You don't turn over the losses of your day; you have chosen to reach beyond winning and losing. And most important, every person with whom you came into some kind of conflict was given a gift: the gift of harmony, of balance, of genuine growth. The only people you couldn't help much were the irate driver and the crazy man in the supermarket. But not everyone can be brought to harmony; that's not your job.

You must first survive.

PART 2

ADVANCED
ATTACK-TICS

IX

Geometry:
The Shape of Conflict

> Geometry is a reflection out
> of the mind of God.
>
> —Johannes Kepler

The shortest distance between you and anything else is a straight line.

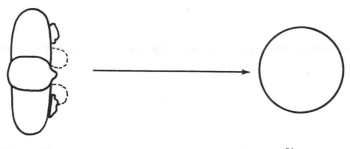

Hungry You   Pizza

Between you and another person, this line runs from heart to heart.

Everything sincere, everything which concerns you deeply, comes and goes along this line. It is the same line on which, as a baby, you moved toward your mother's breast, the line on which she cuddled you to her. It is also the line along which her reprimands came. If you can recall a time when her anger aroused real fear in you, you'll remember that the force came at you hard and straight.

When you're hungry—honest-to-God hungry—you look at your dinner on the line. When you make love with all your heart, you meet your lover on that same line. Ironically, when you're mugged it's that line the mugger follows to get to you and your wallet.

There is geometry in all nature. Human relationships are no exception.

The geometry they taught us in school refers to the relationships of magnitudes in space: points, lines, planes, that sort of thing. For most of us it was just another tedious subject—a dry science which had no connection to the beautiful day outside the schoolroom window. It simply had nothing to do with our lives.

But it did then and it does now.

You ask someone if he got the "point" of what you just

said; you talk of love "triangles," vicious "circles," "square" deals that will keep you from going "flat" broke; you read in the paper about a "pyramid" selling swindle; you watch the "tube" and see a new "star" on the baseball "diamond." To top it off, your President speaks to you from his "Oval" Office about "spiraling" inflation. But the "Pentagon" isn't worried.

The fact is that geometry can be applied on every "plane" of your existence. For instance, Breezy Bill Silvertongue, the car salesman, doesn't know an isosceles triangle from a parallelogram, but he knows the triangle that connects him to Mr. and Mrs. Mark. If he doesn't intuitively sense the three-way relationship between the couple and himself, he'll lose the sale faster than you can say "Dale Carnegie."

When everything is going along smoothly, there's no need to stop and think about geometry. Your intuitive wisdom, sharpened by personal experience, is sufficient to handle whatever situation arises. *But* when you recognize in yourself a persistent inability to respond well to certain types of conflict, it's time to check the geometry of those conflicts.

So as part of the Attack-tics program we're going to give you a quick refresher course in geometry. It's a different kind of geometry from what you learned in school. We'll teach you to see conflict in terms of shapes and forces so that you can stand beyond the reach of your emotions, in a calmer, clearer, more reasonable place—a place where appropriate decisions spontaneously originate. For instance, if you can see Mr. Lynx over in Accounting as a shaped force of nature rather than as a predatory tyrant out to destroy you, you will be able to control your terror and multiply the chances of getting him off your back.

We'll teach you to see geometric structure and harmony in the chaos and conflict around you.

It's not all that hard.

SHAPES OF CONFLICT

In our system, shapes are used to represent certain basic attitudes or qualities. A shape, being an arrangement of lines of force, is a basic, significantly ordered display of energy. This energy determines the nature of the shape, no matter what the dimension.

The relationship of a shape and its energy is obvious when the medium is graspable. A block of stone, for example, is stable precisely because the angles and forces contained within it conspire to keep it that way. If you reshape those lines of force, you alter the basic energy, and vice versa.

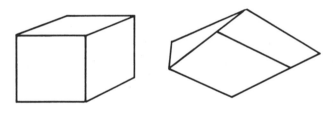

Square Block   Reshaped Block

The reshaped block is no longer quite so stable and its quality is no longer quite so firm. And yet it now possesses other qualities, other lines of force, other energies. It "feels" mobile, ready to spring back.

It's easy to identify energy when the shape is visible; it's only slightly more difficult to assign a shape to a particular kind of energy. For instance, the kids in Mr. Granite's history class know that he's stiff, rigid, and old-fashioned. They sense his energy and assign him a shape: He's a square.

For his part, Mr. Granite is rather proud of his nickname.

He sees himself as solid and dependable. He thinks the little whippersnappers are right for the wrong reasons.

Whoever is right, the sense of the man is understood in basic geometric terms. You can call it "vibes," "sensitivity," "intuition," or "common sense," but we do have an innate sense of the shapes of people and moods.

Think about the shape of the energy you come up against in your daily life. Try to visualize or reexperience a particularly intense exchange with another person, an exchange in which a lot of concentrated energy was expressed. If you were angry, what shape did your anger take? If you were the recipient of anger, in what shape did the incoming anger appear to you? If the exchange was passionate love, what shape was that? If it was intense hatred? jealousy? fear?

If you could step out of an angry exchange and look at it from above, it might look something like this:

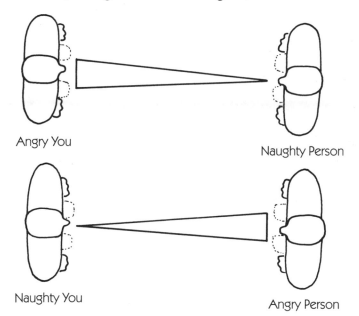

Angry You

Naughty Person

Naughty You

Angry Person

The shape of the attack, the energy which flows from the angry person to the naughty one, is triangular, that sense of an arrowhead piercing the heart. The triangular effect is often heightened by the attacker's using a finger to narrow the focus and point right between the eyes.

It isn't always easy to step outside our conflicts for a bird's-eye view. When you're face to face with an angry person it feels much more as if you're standing in the middle of the train tracks while a freight train bears down on you. You're on that line, and the pointy end of the locomotive is not going to have any trouble going right through you.

And when you're the one who is coming down very hard on someone else, you experience that same sense of focused energy as it bears down on your opponent.

THE THREE SHAPES

Shape is how we'll examine conflict and conflict response, but the shapes are not simply map symbols or schematics. The three shapes we'll be handling actually contain the energy that goes with the action or the response to conflict. As you move along you'll begin to experience what you *feel* like when you become one of the shapes.

The three shapes of conflict response are the triangle, the square, and the circle. As we'll see in more detail, they tend to categorize along these lines:

Fight Back   Do Nothing   Deception
Withdrawal   Parley
                                        Aiki

Let's take them one by one.

THE TRIANGLE

The triangle is most often associated with Fighting Back. Its shape denotes an entering-in, a movement into an attacker's space or, in the case of the attacker, his moving into our space.

But the triangular response can be negative or positive, centered or uncentered. If you switch to the triangular mode and lose your center, you'll be coming across very differently from a centered person in the triangular mode:

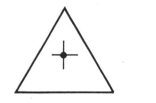 

TRIANGLE

CENTERED	UNCENTERED
dynamic	*aggressive*
entering	*piercing*
purposeful	*one-track*
energetic	*hostile*
forceful	*bullying*
proud	*arrogant*

The person who becomes a centered triangle moves from strength. Try, for a few moments, experiencing the sense of the shape. Stand up and let one of your feet move forward to maintain your balance. Turn your body slightly sideways so that your left or right shoulder points front. Sight along that shoulder and imagine that you are facing another person. Center yourself, bend your knees slightly, and raise your forward arm to shoulder height until you are pointing at the "other person."

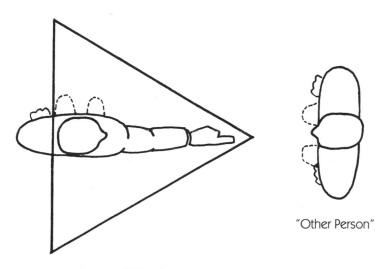

"Other Person"

You as Centered Triangle

Notice how the shape of the triangle begins to suggest inside you the energy, the spirit, of the grounded attack. The thrust forward comes from a strong base. The intention is as clear as the sweep of the sides toward the apex, and your own internal energy begins to be transformed into the "triangular feeling."

Now, bear in mind that we are speaking of the best kind of "good," strong triangular response. Too often we find people Fighting Back with a geometry that looks more like this:

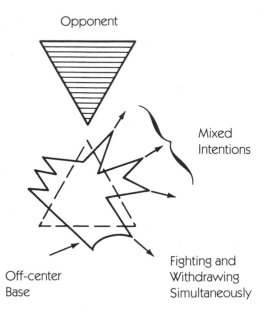

Opponent

Mixed
Intentions

Off-center
Base

Fighting and
Withdrawing
Simultaneously

They flail about in all directions because they don't know what they're all about. Part of them is striking out against a real injustice, part is striking out against old bugaboos from childhood, part is aggressive because of some recent unconnected event, and part is striking out because "that's what you're supposed to do." The base is hysterical, unsupported, unsure of itself, canted at an angle for quick escape in case the conflict gets too hot. And there's even indecision: Part of the person wants to fight and part wants to run like hell.

Against a unified intention—true, grounded triangular energy—that person is almost looking for a rout.

You've begun to feel what *being* a centered triangle is like. You've felt the focus, the flow of energy in that single forward direction. Now all you need to do, besides practicing that feeling, is to remind yourself—right in the middle of a conflict—that you are a triangle (if that is the response you've chosen). You'll be surprised how your body can respond to that command. Notice that you don't talk to yourself in slogans: "Keep your guard up!" "Stop being such a namby-pamby!" Your spirit can't react quickly to that kind of exhortation. Those kinds of expressions are defeatist, complicated, and unusable. The triangular shape contains within it all you need to function.

But the triangular shape or mode of spirit is just as important for Withdrawal as it is for attack. The fact that the apex of the triangle faces away from the conflict means only a change of direction, not a change in spirit or intention. When you choose to Withdraw, you move quickly and efficiently. ("Retreat hell! We're just advancing in another direction!")

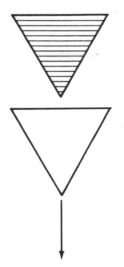

Most people think of Withdrawal as a last chance (if they think of it at all). They get caught. Their "orderly" retreat looks more like the Gauls scrambling before a horde of Visigoths:

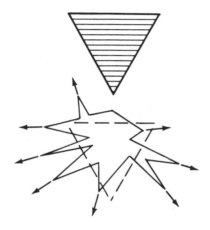

You can almost hear the interior monologue going on inside the person represented by that shape: "Ohmigod! Oh, I hope she doesn't get me! Oh Lord, I'm gonna get it! Maybe if I move faster. Jeez, but I am a loser! Help! I'll run like crazy!"

People who really thrive on attacking people, picking on people, aggressing on people, absolutely love Withdrawals like that one. They'll keep on coming until their victims learn to be more triangular.

By contrast, the interior monologue of the integrated, centered triangle is quite different. In fact, there is almost no interior monologue at all. He or she is in a relaxed state of awareness, an awareness of what's happening, a letting-go, trusting the impulse and going with it. It's the difference between trying to make a marriage "work" and simply being in love with your husband or wife.

Again, just as in the case of the triangle in the attack mode, the triangle in the Withdrawal mode will supply you with all you need to know. Feel like a triangle and you will move, think, and react like one. Your intention will become integrated, and when you feel panic trying to take over you will simply concentrate on the sensation of being a triangle in space and your Withdrawal will be perfect.

Once you have experienced triangularity, check your own sensations against these expressions, which are most often associated with the triangle no matter which direction it is pointed in: entering, exiting, attacking, fighting, running away, avoiding, pursuing, tracking down, struggling, pointing out, trying to make ends meet, escaping, pushing, fleeing, pulling up stakes, going on to another topic, splitting, bugging out, coming down on, zeroing in on.

THE SQUARE

The square is most often associated with the response which we have called Doing Nothing. Its shape denotes stability, protection, standing fast, and safety. And yet it also bears with it the energies of inflexibility and the unwillingness to change.

Like the triangle, the square can be positive or negative; centered or uncentered. If you take on the square shape and lose your center, you will come across very differently from a centered square:

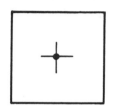   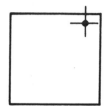

SQUARE

CENTERED	UNCENTERED
solid	*stodgy*
stable	*stuck*
adamant	*piggish*
dependable	*boring*
taking a stand	*afraid to move*

The person who becomes a centered square plays from strength. Try, for a few moments, to experience yourself in the square mode. Experience yourself as a square.

Stand with your feet approximately ten inches apart and your knees slightly bent. Face "squarely" forward. Place one foot forward and get your balance. Find your center:

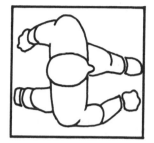

If you allow your arms to swing forward and back (as in the diagram), the area your body covers when viewed from above is roughly a square. It has four right angles, each of which depends on and supports the others. It presents an attacker with four fortified sides. It enables you to turn and face any onrush. Let the sensations of stability and power flood through you as you experience what it is to be a solidly grounded, centered square. Keep your center, and know that you have the right to stand where you are standing, to think as you think. License yourself to hold the beliefs you do, but stand easily. Don't try to grit your teeth and claw the ground with your toes. Your center will hold you fast.

These are the kinds of things you must begin to feel when, in conflict, you choose to Do Nothing. You're not a nebbish, you're not indecisive, you're not at a loss. You are a square —but you've *chosen* to be one!

To sum up the spirit and energy of the square and begin to sense the nature of the transformation, take a look at these square expressions: staying pat, staying put, considering alternatives, reserving judgment, being resolute, "letting him hang himself," waiting it out, being adamant, riding at anchor, weathering the storm, standing fast, holding your own, being dependable, being firm, being staunch.

THE CIRCLE

The circle's spirit is basic to three of the conflict options: Deception, Parley, and Aiki. Each of these options, as we've already seen, is different, but all share many of the aspects of circularity. Moreover, the circularity is of a special kind, whether we're talking about Deception, Parley, or Aiki. It is not circularity for its own sake; it is not circularity for the sake of being slippery or unholdable. It has more to do with the property of a circle that allows you to "roll with the punches" and ultimately to "turn" and see the other person's perspective on things. We all know people we can't get a handle on. They're aloof or repressed or whatever, and we react to them with everything from mild curiosity to real hostility. That's not the spirit of the circle we're talking about.

We're inviting you to become the circle which can accept force, turn with it, and redirect it in a safe direction.

As with the other shapes so far, the circle has a positive, centered side as well as a negative, uncentered side. Remember, the difference in how you come across depends on whether you are dealing from your center.

CIRCLE

CENTERED	UNCENTERED
fluid	*flighty*
can accept force	*can be rolled*
sees all sides	*has no opinions*
fair	*a pushover*
surprising	*tricky*
humane	*neurotic*
reasonable	*a patsy*
accepting	*afraid*

The person who keeps his center while being circular can move and twist and flow and relax like a leaf in the turbulent currents of the river. The uncentered, circular person constantly dodges and weaves and hides and sneaks, petrified of being caught.

That's the difference.

Consider yourself as a circle. Stand comfortably with one foot ahead of the other. Swing your hips from side to side and then allow your arms to follow. It's important not to swing with your arms, but to let your centered hips propel your body, dragging your arms along behind. Drop your center and keep it there. If you can, swing around so that your back foot becomes your front foot. Don't worry about your form, just keep conscious of the feelings of being a circle which can move and roll and flow with anything.

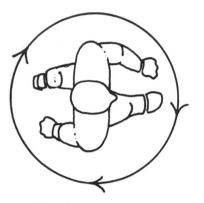

Experience that circle from the inside. Remember how much fun it was when you were a child to spin in endless circles until you collapsed, dizzy and full of laughter. (If most of us tried that today, we'd end up with a mild stroke, at least!)

As you swing from your hips, know that feeling, and know that in conflict you can flow easily with any force. Know that as you turn you can see anything from all sides, that you can perceive anything thrown at you from any of 360 possible directions and still roll or flow with the attack.

Hold on to the memories of those feelings as we next consider the special circularity of the three circular responses.

The Circle of Deception

We are most used to seeing people employ Deception in some strange shape like this:

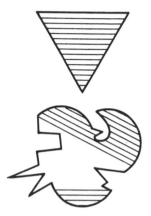

Oh, but can't you hear what's going on in that person's mind? It's like a ten-year-old who's come to school unprepared:

"If she calls on me, I'll walk out! I don't have to take this! If she asks me a spelling word, I'll tell her my younger brother died last night and I didn't have a chance to study. No, she'll never believe that. Oh, God, why didn't I study?" The teacher can already sense from her own center the agony going on in that child. What does she do? She attacks, of course. "Billy, how do you spell 'independent'?"

"Miss Moran, I didn't study that word because my father had this car accident and we had to help him and it was awful . . ." You know the rest. Instead of just getting an F for the day, Billy is now embroiled in a whole drama about lying and morals and ethics, and he wishes he were dead.

So you've gone beyond Billy? You have nothing in common with that ten-year-old? We doubt it. Most of us still approach deception—white lie, gray, or black—with Billy's attitude and spirit. We feel bad for fibbing, we feel guilty about our feelings, and we feel rotten for not being able to deceive better! People are always saying, "I can't do it without blushing," "I can't keep a straight face."

Be circular.

Feel that circle and move with the attack. Get rid of the guilt by knowing that the circle operates in a protective spirit. Attack-tics doesn't ask you to weasel out of a spelling test, or teach you how to lie for fun or profit. We expect you not to misuse your circularity. Your focus should be on the resolution of conflict and the restoration of harmony, not on saving your own skin or putting somebody else down.

If you choose Deception in the face of conflict, be grounded and circular.

The Circle of Parley

How many of you have entered into Parley like this?

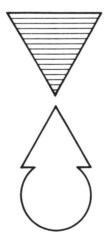

You *mean* to be circular, but you just can't give up your hole card, attacking. You *want* to be reasonable, or you say you're being reasonable, but there's this triangle poking right out at the front of your discussion! If your attacker is perceptive, he may sense the half of you that is circular, but he is forced to respond to the triangle because that is what's threatening him. What's happened is that you have tried to combine, or forgotten to *un*combine, two different conflict responses. For example, you're trying to be reasonable, see the other person's point of view:

> YOU: Yes, I can see your side, Ed, but you don't understand. *Perhaps it's really your problem more than mine . . .*

In the midst of the Parley, the triangle pops out. Something in you wants to zap old Ed, and Ed, if he's any kind of fighter at all, is going to do this:

> ED: Oh yeah? How'd you like this problem! [With that, Ed pokes you in the nose.]

It's difficult because often we're so unaware of what signals we're giving off. We think we're being circular, but two hours after the altercation we realize we were more triangular. It's a question of constantly raising our level of awareness, checking our shape and distilling it down to its essence.

Parley, then, requires that you not give up an arm and a leg, but that you be fluid and flexible and circular enough to turn and see all sides while maintaining your center.

The Circle of Aiki

And then there is the Aiki response, one which demands the most perfect circle you can achieve. If you're lopsided or off center, your response will be as effective as a long-playing record with its hole two inches out of alignment:

This is a blob, not a conflict response. It can't move except the way a cell moves, one pseudopod at a time. While its front is advancing, its rear is waiting its turn to get out of the way of the oncoming attack. It constantly presents vulnerable targets to anyone faster or more agile. It cannot direct or lead, because it doesn't really know where it's going.

A typical example of the lopsided-blob approach to Aiki would be this kind of situation:

MARK: Sheila, I don't like your friends. Not at all.
SHEILA: How can you say that? I mean, well, why would you say a thing like that? Well, from your perspective, sure, I guess— Hey, wait a minute—if you don't like my friends, then what do you like about *me?*

Sheila is just plain off balance. She has gotten herself confused by listening to too many signals at once. She might have done a lot better by simply saying (from her centered circle) "I'm sorry that you feel that way." Then she could have shifted into the square mode and waited for Mark to continue, be more specific, or let his own imbalance work against him.

To sum up the idea, energy, and spirit of the circle, let's review some of the phrases, words, and expressions which are common to that shape:

CIRCLE: (Parley) hash things out, discuss, enter into a give-and-take, compromise, go halfway with somebody, trade, go round and round, give a few inches, "you scratch my back and I'll scratch yours," work out a deal, come up with something mutually acceptable.

Circle: Parley

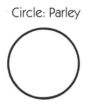

CIRCLE: (Deception) tell a white lie, change the focus, bring up short, tell half the truth, put the ball back in his court, change the subject, interrupt the conflict.

Circle: Deception

CIRCLE: (Aiki) enter in and turn, empathize, join with, go with the flow, roll with the punch, see it from his perspective, be the water not the rock, walk a mile in his shoes, redirect his arguments, help him see what's really happening, "walk around in his skin."

Circle: Aiki

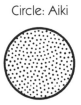

To be sure, there is no easy road to Attack-tics. But, if you practice identifying with and "owning" the three basic shapes *while retaining your center,* you'll have gone much further on the path toward effective conflict management.

UPPING THE ANTE

All along we've spoken of the three shapes as if each were totally independent of the others. In a sense that is true, but in another sense it is not exactly true. You don't put on a triangle the way you put on a new shirt or blouse. You don't take it off again to become a square or a circle. In effect, although the shapes are separate, you carry them with you all the time. At any given moment in the day one shape predominates, but the others are right there, available to you if you should need them. For example, in the square mode you would actually look something like this:

In this case the square predominates, but the circle and the triangle are still there in case a fast shift is in order—from

square to circle—

or—

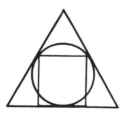

—from circle to triangle.

The point which underlies all this is that everyone is always something, some shape. Some mode is predominating. Though shifts from one mode to another are usually subtle, most people can be easily categorized, because they slip into one mode more often than the others. There are those who prowl through life as "tigers," following the points of their triangles, always looking for a "kill" of some kind. On the other hand, there are those who are always looking for an escape clause, their apexes always pointing away from conflict. The squares, as we've seen, tend to stand adamant and resolute; if uncentered, they can be as stubborn as mules.

Those who tend to be circular more often than any other shape can be viewed in any of six possible ways: deceitful/creative, reasonable/talkative, or confluent/pushover.

Bear in mind that you have many options and you carry them around with you at all times. Don't get trapped in one mode to the exclusion of the others.

For instance, what would you say your mode is right now as you read this book? If you're disagreeing with everything we've said, or looking for typographical errors to justify your dislike of Attack-tics, you are clearly in the triangular mode. The circle and the square are at rest inside you.

If you're anxious about what we're saying, and would rather not understand or practice it, you're still in the triangular mode, aimed *away from* what you're experiencing.

If you are reading along quietly, waiting to see what the bottom line is—what is this Attack-tics all about, anyway? —then you're resting comfortably in the square mode. Give Dobson and Miller enough time and they'll either hang themselves or convince you.

If you're reading actively, questioning yourself and us, agreeing here, disagreeing there, then you're in a circle, in Parley with the text and the concepts. You're still in the circular mode, but uncentered, if you're reading along and slipping past the ideas by telling yourself how little you need all this stuff, because everything's just fine except for the fact that you keep losing control in your conflicts and your wife just threw you out of the house, but you're okay. And anyway, who cares! If you're in confluence, you're not necessarily convinced of the correctness of our approach, but for the duration of your reading you're trying on the ideas and flowing with them to experience what they feel like. You're playing a little game called As If. You read or do something as if it were so. Then, when you're finished, you decide whether it is right or wrong for you.

You should begin being acutely aware at all times of what shape you are experiencing. At first it will seem that you are all three or two or six others you've invented for yourself: "I feel like a rhomboid today," "I'm somewhere between a parallelogram and a rectangle . . ." As you think about it, and as you take stock of what is really going on, you will discover that whether you are in conflict or not, you are taking on some aspect or aspects of one of the three shapes.

Just as important, when you are engaging in any interpersonal relationship, whether that relationship is conflictual or pacific, you should know which mode you're in and which mode you "ought" to be in. Only you can decide what "ought" means, using the hints we've provided.

Learn to use your new knowledge of geometry to guide you in your conflict situations. As your ex-spouse is heaping opprobrium on your head, say the words to yourself and you'll save that head: "Be a circle."

We think you'll find the repetition of the shapes far more helpful than mumbling to yourself: "If she says one more thing, I'll really let her have it!" or "My time will come, boy!" or "I don't have to let him get away with this!"

Your body will respond, your spirit will respond, and you will do the "right" thing, because your center will not let you fail.

DEALING ON THE LINE

We began this chapter by saying that the shortest distance connecting you to everyone else is a straight line. The shapes of attacker and responder work out their conflicts on that line. Let's look at the geometry of the line itself.

Any serious attack moves from the attacker to the target along a straight line:

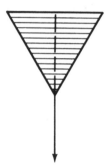

We say any "serious" attack because attacks which are not serious don't concern us here. An attack without any force behind it, an attack which is idle or only half thought out, an attack which is unsupported—none of those need bother you. You simply step calmly out of the way or flick your wrist and those attacks disappear in a mist of inconsequentiality.

No, it's serious attacks we need deal with. And serious attacks travel across and along this straight line. Behind them is a great deal of intention. The attacker is totally committed to his or her attack; ironically, it is that total commitment which makes your job of responding so simple. For example, if a man runs at you with all his force and you step out of the way, he's going to keep on running until he can dig his heels into the pavement and stop. *That's* total commitment! However, if that same man walks slowly at you and you step out of the way, he can immediately come at you again and be all over your back. Thus, *the stronger the attack, the easier it is for you to handle.*

Hard to believe?

We're asking you to accept that your survival prognosis is far better if somebody *really* jumps all over you. It happens to be true. The more committed your attacker is, the easier it is for you to handle him if you're centered. Since birth we've been trained to hope that the boss, wife, husband, son, daughter, best friend, enemy, bully will pull their punches and come down on us only a little bit. But look at that person as the triangle in our diagram above. See him coming straight at you along that line. Imagine the force, will, and intention all focused along that arrow. Know, then, that when someone attacks you along that line, you have 358 directions you can go in to deal safely and simply with the attacker—every direction, in fact, except north or south.

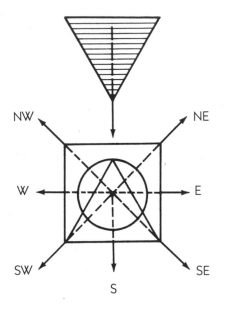

North will bring you into a head-on collision with your attacker; south will force you to outrun him. But you do have 358 safe directions you can go in with a minimum of effort, and that doesn't even take into consideration the slightly more complicated use of Aiki (north and south) which could add 2 extra degrees to your life choices!

Okay, let's leave the navigation class for a moment and look again at that line which connects you to your attacker. Notice that it is straight. It connects your heart to his or her heart. He or she may feel that the heart is not involved, but you must remember that it is or you'll lose sight of the protective spirit. You can try to deal with people obliquely, hiding from them or dealing dishonestly with them, but the *real* direct line still exists:

Triangle to square:

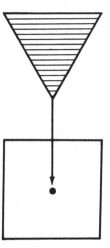

Triangle to circle:

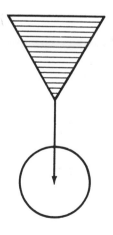

No matter which shapes are present, the line continues to exist between people in their relationships. The difficulty begins when they misperceive that line or pretend it isn't there. To go back to an earlier metaphor, let's take Robin Hood and Little John. That log bridge on which they stand is a physical representation of the "imaginary line" which connects two or more people in any relationship. They can't get off their log without getting wet. Neither can we. To deal on any other line is, at the very least, counterproductive:

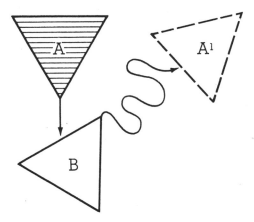

A¹ is B's *idea* of A, not the *actual* A. In this case A is attacking B, but B is distracted or fighting some other imagined fight. The result is that A has a clear shot right down the pike into B's center. All B has to do is get back on the line to engage in the conflict. For example, let's imagine that A is the phone company and B is a young woman named Maggie. Maggie can best be described as "semiliberal" in her politics; she has spent some time supporting various causes. When the phone company comes down on her for nonpayment, threatening to cut off her service, Maggie immediately shifts into the triangular mode, ready to fight back. Like most of us, she distrusts large corporations, and she sees this fight with the phone people as a struggle of humankind against monolith. The phone company, on the other hand, sees the event as a simple question of nonpayment for services rendered. The fact that their computer is in error is not yet known to them.

During the fight with the business-department supervisor, Maggie goes into an uncentered triangular tirade:

> MAGGIE: You people don't give a damn about us! You've sold out! You're ripping off an entire country and worse than that, you're even interfering in the internal affairs of foreign countries. I'm going to get the ACLU after you!

She goes on. The net result of her bravura performance is that she angers the business rep to the point where reasonable discussion isn't even possible. The company cuts off her service.

You are perfectly free to agree with Maggie, but the fight wasn't about whether ITT interferes in South America. It was about whether or not Maggie had paid last month's phone bill! Anyway, the business rep had a job to do, and did so by staying on a single direct line: Was the bill paid or not? If Maggie had dealt on *that* line, she might have caused the business department to review its computer accuracy and the ways customers are dealt with. Instead, she fought on her own line—a line connected to no one except the board of directors of the corporation. And *they* weren't around to hear!

The key is to *find the direct line, stay on it, and respond appropriately.*

Otherwise, like Maggie, you'll only end up fighting yourself.

To increase your expertise with Attack-tics, begin to visualize the lines which connect you to the people you deal with. Remember that the lines are not restricted to husbands and wives, bosses, and co-workers, but connect to everybody.

To sum up: Geometry is a way of looking at what happens in our daily conflicts. It clears up and makes definite the dynamics of interaction, pointing out the shape to take and the course to follow if we are to survive.

Know which shape predominates—be the circle, the square, the triangle—and use it in the protective spirit.

X

Multiple Attack

The hurricane of miracles blows perpetually. Day
and night the phenomenon surges around us on
all sides, and (not least marvelous) all without
disturbing the majestic tranquility of the Cre-
ation. This tumult is harmony.

—Victor Hugo
William Shakespeare

Multiple attack is exactly what it says it is. It is a situation
in which you are beset not with one single attacker, but with
a number of them. These are the events of conflict which
really try our capacity to handle aggression. Multiple attack
is frightening.

Traditionally, as we've mentioned before, we've been
taught to feel that big is powerful and small is weak. The
extension of that lesson is that the many are powerful, the
few are weak. Therefore, if little old us is caught facing big
old them, we are led to expect our defeat. As we'll see, that
is plainly not the case. Recent military history is too full of
examples of guerrilla forces overpowering armies of superior
numbers and weaponry.

The first step is to realize that number works *against* the numerous as easily as it works *for* the numerous. For instance, though you may have five hundred soldiers up against only fifty soldiers, you must feed, clothe, arm, minister to, organize, and orchestrate ten times the number of your opponent. You may have more firepower, but you must provide the ammunition and make sure that firepower is directed correctly. Meanwhile, your smaller enemy is relatively free to range about, making inroads on your lines of supply. In addition, fifty make less noise than five hundred and can deploy faster and hide more effectively.

So it is crucial for you to remember that when you're up against a multiple attack, you still have all four aces in your deck; they have had to split theirs up among themselves!

What are some examples of multiple attack? Two parents aggressing on one child, three colleagues harassing one worker, a board of directors coming down hard on a particular member, five neighbors ganging up on one family, a friend who wants you to go in one direction while another friend wants you to go in the opposite direction. If you stop to think about it, we face almost as many multiple attacks in a month as we do of the one-on-one variety.

Let's look at the geometry of some types of multiple attack:

1. THE SANDWICH

In this instance, A and A^1 are attacking B. Like any really good attackers, they surround B with their assault, minimizing B's escape options. In interpersonal terms, you know the situation: Edgar says you're selfish. Then, just as you're dealing with Edgar's attack, Randy comes up and says you're

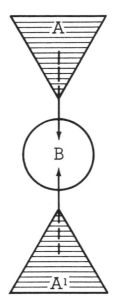

insensitive. Just as you're dealing with Randy, Edgar redoubles his attack by telling you you're a rotten administrator. Neither of them may be right, but they've sure got you coming and going. How do you handle that?

Notice in the drawing that A and A¹ have both aimed their respective attacks right along that line toward B's center. But what if B isn't there? What if all of a sudden B's circle moves?

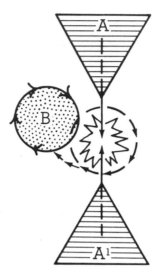

Depending on B's speed and agility, A and A¹ will run right
into each other! To the degree that their attacks are serious
and committed, their own momentum will carry them along
the line to which they are committed. B is then in a relatively
safe position from which he can deal with their second attack.

Let's see how it works in verbal terms.

EDGAR: Frank, you were really insulting last night!

RANDY: I hope you're proud of yourself, Frank!

EDGAR: How could you have been so mean!

RANDY: I know that Helen's tightfisted, but you didn't have
to tell her to her face!

FRANK: (Being circular.) I know you two are upset about
what I did, and maybe I need your help. Edgar, tell
me, how would you have handled Helen's being late
with her share of the rent?

RANDY: (Still rushing along.) I'll tell you how *I* would have handled things.

EDGAR: Wait, Randy. He asked me. For one thing, I wouldn't have done it in front of all the roommates.

RANDY: That wasn't it at all, Edgar! It was Frank's whole attitude about it. So ironic and nasty.

EDGAR: Irony's the only way to get through to Helen. I just wouldn't have done it in front of everybody.

FRANK: (Looking for the resolution.) I guess there's a whole lot more anger tied up in the Helen problem than I realized. Let's see if we can't find some common ground we can agree on and then go from there.

Frank wasn't just lucky, He followed the diagram perfectly, moved his circle in a centered manner, and got out of the Sandwich Randy and Edgar had prepared for him. Obviously, Edgar and Randy were equally upset about Helen's slow rent payments, but they took their anger out on Frank. Frank helped them by letting them run headlong into each other. That collision caused the truth to surface and then made it possible for all three to move toward a resolution. Frank allowed all of this to happen by not taking the personal attacks personally. His center helped him stay out of the battle zone.

2. THE TUG OF WAR

Virtually the same thing happens when you're in the situation where two opposing forces are pulling you in opposite directions:

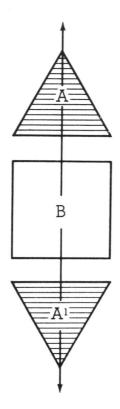

If you think about it geometrically, A and A¹ are actually pulling each other! Just as in the preceding example, they were attacking each other. The fact that B is in the way can be viewed as an accident of history rather than a tragedy. Of course, if B continues to stand in a resolute square his arms will be pulled out of his sockets. He must be able to capitalize on the concept that A and A¹ really want each other. He visualizes himself as a rope and lets the two attackers pull against each other. As he experiences this Tug of War, he feels that A¹ is stronger than A. So he becomes a triangle pointing in the same direction as A¹, and look what happens now:

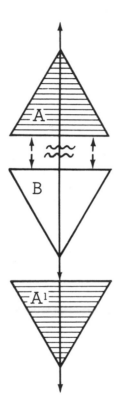

With trumpets and fanfare, we have two triangles pulling against one triangle! As we'll soon see, when B and A¹ have the configuration moving in the direction of A¹, B can shift into a circle and get out of the way so that A and A¹ can experience what's really happening.

Let's take a classic example of the Tug of War in a real-life situation: the college-age son torn between a mother who wants him to go into liberal arts and a father who wants him to go into engineering. Trite, perhaps, but so common as to provide millions of families with a lifetime supply of conflict.

Just as in our geometric diagram, the father and mother are actually two triangles pulling against each other. For the parents, it's a win/lose situation disguised under the banner of "What's Best for Junior." Unfortunately for Junior, he doesn't understand adult power struggles; he experiences the pulls as separate and directed at him personally. Ultimately, only Junior will know what's best for Junior, so he'll have to learn how to deal with the geometry of the situation.

First both triangles pull against the square:

> MOM: Trust me, son, I really do know what's best for you. A liberal-arts degree will allow you to go into all sorts of different fields. It'll make you a well-rounded person.
>
> DAD: And an engineering degree'll get you a good job and a good salary. If you know what's good for you, you'll sign up for engineering as soon as you can get your name on the dotted line.

Junior stands still, keeps his center, and waits out the conflict until he begins to feel that one side is stronger than the other—not necessarily better for him, but stronger in terms of the force exerted. His father's voice is getting louder, his examples more numerous, his face redder, so Junior slowly turns into a triangle aimed in the same direction as the engineering pole:

> JUNIOR: I think Dad's got a good point about the freedom of choice within the structure of engineering as well as the unlimited job opportunities.

DAD: Damn right I do!
MOM: What's *that* supposed to mean!

Now when Junior is certain his mother is almost on the ropes, he becomes a circle and gets out of the way:

JUNIOR: Dad, why don't *you* explain it to Mom? I'm not as sure about the facts.
MOM: I don't want anything explained to me!
DAD: That's your problem. Your mind is already made up and you won't listen to simple facts!
MOM: What about you? Sitting there and telling our son to toss his life away on facts and figures! What makes you so right all the time? I raised him while you were out selling all the time. You don't even know who he is! How can you advise him what to do?
DAD: I was out all the time making money to support the two of you! You babied him all along, and now you want him to graduate with a degree that doesn't mean a thing! What gives you the right any more than me to tell him what to do?

The fight has now boiled down (or up, if you prefer) to its essence: Who has the power, right, or authority to govern Junior's choice? All the flimflammery of engineering versus liberal arts (even though they may be sincere opinions) has been stripped away. Depending on the boy's relationship with his parents up to this time, he can now help them find some kind of resolution through Aiki:

JUNIOR: Mom and Dad, I've listened to both of you very carefully. Now tell me if I've heard right. It seems that you both love me very much.
MOM: Of course.
DAD: Of course.

JUNIOR: But it also seems that the argument you've been having has to do with who is going to have the power to choose my future for me, not whether I'll be an engineer or a poet. Maybe we ought to deal with *that* first.

DAD: Well, of course, the choice is finally up to you, son. I never meant it wasn't.

MOM: Why, yes, of course it's up to you, dear.

JUNIOR: I love you both very much.

Junior's parents could have kept the fight alive; there are many people who refuse to see what conflicts are really about. But they accepted his point and learned from it. They learned that their son would no longer play the victim in their fights, that he was well on his way to being an adult and wouldn't cover up their real motives any longer. Paradoxically, the gift he gave them was the gift of direct confrontation, the gift of having it out mother-to-father rather than mother-to-son-to-father and vice versa. Their ability to handle those direct conflicts will determine where their relationship goes from here.

It's almost as important to consider for a moment what did *not* happen. Junior did not insult his parents; he didn't go screaming out of the house; he didn't get bullied into choosing a future just to keep his parents' marriage in one piece; and he didn't go away from the scene feeling pitifully small. Instead, he was a peacemaker, promoting harmony.

Every day professional arbitrators do what Junior did; good bosses try to handle factions; teachers step between playground pugilists. And it doesn't matter whether it's two against one or two hundred against one. The same principles and solutions apply.

3. I'VE GOT THEM SURROUNDED

Of course, not all multiple attacks lay out as easily as the Sandwich and the Tug of War. Some look more like this:

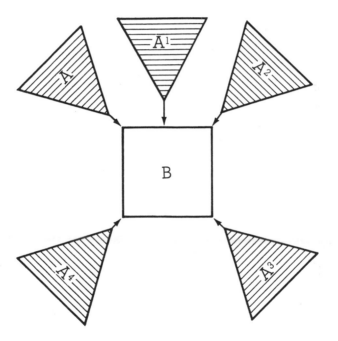

So far as we can see, B is surrounded by five attackers. There he is, Doing Nothing, and the whole world, it seems, is out to do him in.

Wrong.

Reframe it. Look at the picture again this way:

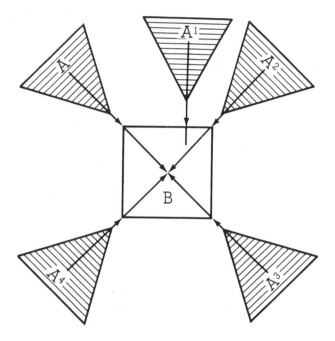

Look at what's actually happening, if you can forget that poor B is beset by enemies and problems and attackers. A and A^3 are pushing against each other, A^2 and A^4 are pushing against each other, and A^1 is setting the whole thing off balance! In truth, all of the A's *require* B's presence or they'd fall in a heap on the floor!

All B needs to do is become a circle and begin to spin slowly in either direction. Because of the nature of the force exerted by the attackers, they'll start to slip and slide into one another:

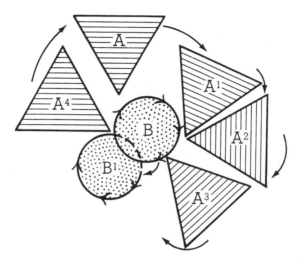

A slides towards A¹, A¹ and A² collide and head toward A³, while A⁴ slips into A. As soon as the chain reaction begins, B slips down and out, coming up behind A⁴, where he can shove the whole chorus line into a jumble. Once the innocent victim, he is now behind the whole crowd, directing it wherever he needs to. The process can be repeated no matter how many oppressors there are.

Now notice that after B is out of the middle he's essentially come out like this:

If the A's want to redirect their aggression at B, they'll virtually have to climb through one another in order to reach him. B can deal with A⁴ and handle him, but A and the others must get past A⁴ to attack B. That's the prime rule for handling *any* multiple attack, and especially "I've Got Them Surrounded": *Always keep an attacker between you and another attacker.* In other words, use one attacker to shield you from another.

It's complicated, so let's retrace the course of action you take when you're surrounded. First, you center yourself and become circular. Second, you start turning from your center. Third, as the attackers begin to shove one another around, you slip down and behind them, directing their ultimate course. Fourth, you keep at least one attacker between you and all the rest. *Throughout the maneuver, you never allow yourself to believe you're surrounded.*

You've probably been involved in many attacks of this kind. See if you can remember how you handled one of them. How did you respond? How did you feel? What was the outcome? Watch how Linda handles one.

Linda is thirty, a second-grade teacher in a middle-class community. She believes in developing the whole child in her classroom, and she doesn't stress skills so much as she tries to install self-confidence and encourage curiosity. In an era of shrinking job markets and increasing educational accountability, many middle-class parents have turned their attention to their children's acquisition of skills. Linda is in a bind. She believes in what she's doing, but if she does it, she'll be flying in the face of the expressed needs of the students' parents.

She does what she believes in.

At first Linda gets away with it. Gradually, however, she becomes aware of a certain amount of sniping behind her back—circular attacks by a few parents. She knows that this cannot go on indefinitely, so she moves in on a straight line to bring the attacks into direct confrontation. She calls a meeting of her students' parents to discuss the educational program she's implemented.

It's a frightening array that faces Linda that evening. A dozen sets of parents have shown up. Of the dozen, fully ten pairs of parents are out for Linda's hide. To return to our geometric picture, Linda is surrounded by twenty triangles all aimed at her center. The other four individuals are, for the most part, squares, waiting to see what happens.

Linda centers herself. The act of centering helps her remember that the parents really aren't out to get her. They're anxious about their children, worried that maybe they've done a poor job of child-raising, troubled by their own economic futures, and generally distressed by the world they've grown up in. These parents are united only by the desire to make their children smart—but not just as smart as every other child! In a few years these kids will be competing against one another for admission to college, law school, etc. Thus, as in the drawing, these triangles actually *need* Linda in the middle to keep them from fighting one another.

After the opening remarks, the battle is on. Mrs. Anderson is the bravest and the most outspoken.

> MRS. ANDERSON: We have five demands which we want implemented immediately or we'll be forced to institute proceedings against you to replace you as the teacher of our children. It is nothing personal, Linda, but we are quite adamant about it.

Linda pays attention to her own breathing to help her keep her center and keep from screaming back, "Look here, sister, I'm a professional teacher and I know what's best for your children!" She realizes that Mrs. Anderson has, in the best tradition of aggressors, attacked with such force that she has almost lost her balance. Linda's best course is to become circular in order to let Mrs. Anderson slide toward the other attackers.

> LINDA: Thank you, Mrs. Anderson, for your candor. Have the other parents read the list of demands?
> MRS. ANDERSON: Uh, I think some have. I'm not sure about all.

LINDA: Why don't you read them for us?

MRS. ANDERSON: Well, okay. First, we want one hour per child per day of reading instruction. Second, we want the same amount of time spent on arithmetic. Third, we want less emphasis on art and music. Fourth, we want a study-skills course, and fifth, we want regular achievement and diagnostic testing.

LINDA: Thank you. I can certainly appreciate your concern. I wish more parents were as concerned as you all are. Is everyone satisfied with the five points Mrs. Anderson has enumerated?

It's worth noting here that Linda might well have gone to the mat on all five points and screamed about the necessity for art and music, etc. Instead, she turned quietly from her center, letting Mrs. Anderson face the others head on.

MRS. BARBER: I'm not so sure about cutting back on art and music.

MRS. CARPENTER: Who needs art and music to get a job? That's what we're talking about here, isn't it?

MRS. BARBER: Is it?

MR. DIXON: What about all that testing? Lonnie doesn't test all that well . . .

MRS. BARBER: I want to know about what the purpose of a good education is!

MRS. EDISON: Testing is very important these days.

MRS. ANDERSON: People! We're losing sight of what we came here for!

LINDA: Yes, Mrs. Anderson is quite right. You came here because you were concerned about your children.

Linda, having slipped out of the way, is now directing from behind Mrs. Anderson. Mrs. Anderson appears to have caught on to what Linda's up to, but the other parents, like the geometric shapes, are too busy bumping into one another to help her out.

> MRS. ANDERSON: I'd like to hear what Linda has to say to these five demands.

That's a nice attempt on Mrs. Anderson's part to try to realign the attack at the target. But if Linda can hang on to her circle, redirecting the new thrust, she'll come out okay.

> LINDA: I respect the need that lies behind the demands, but inasmuch as I am teaching *your* children, it's more important what *you* think about them. I could go on and on and on, but it would still boil down to what you want for your children. I need your input.
>
> MRS. BARBER: I still want to know what's the point of my son's education.
>
> MRS. CARPENTER: It doesn't have anything to do with painting pictures and singing songs, I'll tell ya.
>
> MR. DIXON: Why should Lonnie have to be tested all the time?
>
> MRS. EDISON: My George didn't used to test very well, but he's been practicing . . .
>
> LINDA: There seem to be a number of divergent opinions here.
>
> MRS. BARBER: But you're the professional. What do *you* say?

Now, if Linda shifts into the square mode and comes out with her own five-point program, she'll end up giving Mrs. Anderson a very specific target. Linda stays circular.

LINDA: Thank you, Mrs. Barber, but I can't really respond to you the way you'd like. What we've got here is a group of extremely concerned, extremely troubled parents. You're concerned because you want the best for your children; you're troubled because no one really knows what will be best for your children in ten or twelve years. We're in the middle of an area of opinion, some informed opinion, some emotional opinion. I can lend all of you some texts which I think are important, and we can meet regularly to discuss them, but I can't stand here and tell you you're right or wrong. As we go along, we can take Mrs. Anderson's points one by one, and see if we can reach a consensus.

Linda makes sure to go back to the list of demands, because Mrs. Anderson is the triangle she's keeping between herself and the rest of the potential attackers.

The outcome of the multiple attack upon Linda was that she gave herself the opportunity to teach the parents of her students. She held a series of group discussions and appointed Mrs. Anderson chairperson in order to keep the focus on learning rather than on her teaching. By the end of the year the group of concerned parents had been *led* to understand why it was important to train competent learners rather than competent test-takers and skill-manipulators. Linda "won," but so did the parents—and so did the children. A potentially disharmonious situation, filled with rancor, turned into a full life experience for everyone concerned.

It doesn't matter whether the fight is between teachers and parents, department heads and staff, or chairmen of the board and board members. The same geometry and dynamics are operative.

The problem is that most of us in those situations rant and rave and shout about our rights and opinions. We rattle the bars on the cages of our egos until somebody tells us we're great people. We think that if we Fight Back we'll be noticed and appreciated and loved.

It just isn't that way at all.

Even if a group of attackers appears totally united, totally agreed on one single point, the geometry still works. If all twenty parents had agreed on the five points, Linda's action of slipping out of the middle would still have brought out the distrusts and insecurities in her attackers. They might have agreed on cutting out music and art, but there would still have been disagreement in some other area—enough to let Linda come up and begin to lead the group toward harmony.

And, no, you're not dividing and conquering. *Linda conquered nothing* except her own old fear of failure. She worked in the protective spirit and helped each of her potential tormentors toward a better understanding of what he or she really wanted. Had she been dishonest, had she gloated over her victory, those same parents would have felt that they were being had, and Linda wouldn't have lasted through the semester. Attack-tics isn't a shuck; it isn't for demagogues.

To sum up: Responding to a multiple attack—the Sandwich, the Tug of War, and "I've Got Them Surrounded"—is not easy the first time you are involved in one. You'll have to concentrate hard on your center to keep from being "convinced" by your old sensibilities that you must become triangular and poke out at each attacker. You must learn to breathe out slowly and relax so that you can reframe what your eyes tell you is a million screaming warriors trying to set fire to your Fort Apache.

In a strange way, you'll soon discover that multiple attacks and your harmonious resolution of them are the most rewarding of all. They make you feel the best about your ability to handle the rough edges which come at you in life.

XI

But Isn't It Hard to Change?

And he changed his behavior
before them, and feigned himself
mad in their hands. . . .

—I Samuel 21.13

Yes.

But it isn't as hard or as traumatic as David's change in
the face of Achish, the King of Gath. Attack-tics doesn't ask
you to feign madness. And, conversely, if you do try Attack-
tics, people will not notice your halo or stop you on the street
to ask you why you look so confident. Handsome men and
women won't fall all over themselves trying to get the key to
your door.

But you won't need all that attention any more. You'll
feel a new sense of connection to yourself and to the
human race. You'll spend a lot less time worrying yourself about what you've done or not done. You won't feel
as guilty or uncontrolled as you used to. You won't feel
like a victim.

Okay, but how to begin? You've spent a good many years
dealing one way with conflict, and it is going to be difficult

trying another. After fighting your siblings and your parents and your colleagues for umpteen years, how do you all of a sudden become calm and centered and circular or square?

It's simple. You do it.

A psychiatrist we know had as a patient a kleptomaniac, who was compelled to keep on stealing. During his first hour on the analytic couch, the kleptomaniac said, "I want to stop stealing!" The psychiatrist, a very wise man, thought for half a second and said, "So? Stop stealing."

At first glance, one wonders who is the patient and who is the doctor.

But, if you think about it, what's wrong with the M.D.'s approach? The kleptomaniac says he wants to stop. Simply expressing that desire should be enough, shouldn't it? He knows what the problem is, and the M.D. has given him the solution: stop stealing.

If the patient can't stop, what's the matter with him? Is it a failure of will? A failure of the superego to control the subconscious? A failure of the psychiatrist to help the patient? No self-discipline? A breakdown of law and order?

It has to do with one key word: *want.* What do you want? The answer is never easy. Do you really want it? That answer is even harder to come by.

We should be on fairly safe semantic ground if we say that the kleptomaniac wants to stop stealing. But he says he can't. Something in him simply won't let him stop. We must assume that something in him doesn't want to stop, because if *all* of him really wanted to stop, he would. It's the psychiatrist's job to help him find what that other want is so that when he says, "I want to stop stealing," *all of him* wants to stop stealing.

If you say you really want to stop "losing fights" or you want to stop being a bully or you want to stop arguing all the time, you'll get pretty much the same advice from us as our friend with the sticky fingers got from his shrink: "So stop."

But first you've got to be honest, painfully so, and find out which part of you doesn't want to quit. There's no biological demand that you fight every time somebody honks a horn at you at a traffic light; there's no physiological need to yell when you're yelled at; there's no economic necessity that requires every victim to counterattack at every jab in its direction.

So somewhere inside you must enjoy:

FIGHTING

LOSING

DISHARMONY

(Who, *me?* How could I *enjoy* all that bad stuff?)

We use the word "enjoy" very loosely. No one actually enjoys losing. But something inside each of us requires some kind of perilous equilibrium which depends on old patterns of conflict, victimization, loss, etc. These old patterns give us the feeling that we are balanced, even at the cost of our mental health. Consciously we do *want* to stop them. Whatever else they may do for us, fights make us uneasy, make us feel barbaric, make us afraid of losing control. Nevertheless, we keep on fighting. We try to balance our imbalance by making these kinds of destructive choices.

For example, take Roy—"normal" in every respect, yet deep within himself he doesn't think he's a very worthwhile person. He's a nice guy, and everybody on the commuter car knows him by face if not by name. Roy's got a wife, two children, a mortgage, and an elderly mother who lives with the family.

Roy is a loser.

Not the kind people write movies about. Nothing too tragic or too upsetting. It's just that whenever a big conflictual event—tennis or business or social—comes up, Roy tries like hell and comes up unhappy. He either overextends and throws an angry fit or loses confidence midway and starts feeling sorry for himself.

When we first met Roy, he told us with all sincerity that he was tired of "choking up" and losing his cool whenever he faced a conflict. He was tired of the constant friction at home, the bickering and stormy confrontations. He didn't "enjoy" the conflicts at the office, either, and he wanted to be able to play a tennis match just once without worrying about having to prove himself.

Roy wanted to win.

He wasn't overjoyed by our "digression" on zero-sum and non-zero-sum games, but he agreed that, yes, life had misinformed him about winning and losing. He told us he'd like to "succeed" in the Attack-tics spirit and mode.

Roy learned all the concepts very quickly. He didn't know it then, but although his conscious mind understood what we were teaching him, something deeper was having a very hard time.

When he began to use Attack-tics, he managed his first few conflicts well. He reported back to us that some people he'd never been able to "handle" were now eminently manageable and that he was euphoric over his success. His fears that he would sound phony had all gone by the boards.

But soon Roy began to feel ill at ease with what had happened to him. His initial euphoria was wearing off. Gradually he fell back into his old modes of behavior. To get himself off the hook, he blamed Attack-tics, saying, "It's okay for the small stuff, but not for the really important conflicts." He brought us stories designed to show us where our system failed. He began a number of circular attacks on us, such as "I don't want to tell you you're wrong but . . ." and so on.

Using Attack-tics, we moved in on Roy on a straight line to get him to confront us.

> US: Roy, what is it you want to tell us? You're beating all around the bush and trying to be helpful, but it's obvious you're hiding something.
>
> ROY: It doesn't work!
>
> US: Give us some more help. Be more specific.
>
> ROY: You guys don't know what you're talking about.
>
> US: That's possible, but you've got to tell us where we're wrong.
>
> ROY: Well, for one thing you've completely left out the simple fact that sometimes it's just a whole lot of fun to fight. There's nothing wrong with fighting. Sometimes it feels good to get it out of your system!
>
> US: Tell us about the fight that felt good. The therapeutic fight. [We were genuinely interested, so shifting into Aiki was no problem.]
>
> ROY: Well, like when the guy promised me the TV set would be repaired by Saturday and I went down Saturday morning and he said it wouldn't be ready until Monday. I really let him have it. Usually maybe I'd just nod and say, "okay," but this time I got hopping mad.
>
> US: Who attacked you in that situation?
>
> ROY: Nobody. The son of a bitch didn't have my TV set ready.
>
> US: So *you* attacked *him?*
>
> ROY: I was furious. Didn't I have a right to be?
>
> US: Of course you had a right to be angry. But Attack-tics is a self-defense form, not a way of attacking shoddy craftsmen. Give us an example of how our approach let you down when *you* were attacked.
>
> ROY: Well, my wife yelled at me last night because I hadn't done some stupid job or other, and I yelled right back.

I wasn't going to make a circle for her, boy. And it felt
good to give her back what she gave me, let me tell ya.

US: What did she yell at you about?

ROY: I'd promised to clean out the tropical fish tank last
week and I'd been too busy.

US: What did she say? Specifically . . .

ROY: She said, "Clean out the goddamned fish tank or all the
goddamned fish are gonna die!"

US: What did you yell back?

ROY: "I'll clean the tank when I'm goddamned good and
ready!"

US: Then what happened?

ROY: It got hot and heavy. She called me a lazy selfish bas-
tard, and I called her a cretin and told her if she cared
so much about the fish she could clean them herself!

US: How did it end up?

ROY: She slammed out of the den and cried on her bed for
a while.

US: But you felt good because you'd won?

ROY: I'd gotten it out of my system! That's the trouble with
Attack-tics. It doesn't let you get it out of your system.
That's not natural.

US: Were you just angry about being yelled at about the fish
tank?

ROY: No . . . I'd had a bad day. The fish tank was just the
last straw.

US: What happened at the office that you were still angry
about?

ROY: My department head told me to start all over on a job
I'd been doing for a week and a half.

US: Why didn't you get it out of your system by yelling
back at him?

ROY: And lose my job? With *him* I was circular.

US: But you *did* fight back at your wife?

ROY: I know it isn't fair, but I was furious.

US: What was the first thing you said to your wife after the
fight? Can you remember?

ROY: I said I was sorry. That was only fair.

US: What were you sorry about?

ROY: That I'd yelled at her even though it wasn't all her fault. And for some of the things I called her.

US: Did she accept your apology?

ROY: She wasn't too happy about things. I guess she did.

US: How did you feel then?

ROY: A little ridiculous.

US: And when your boss yelled at you, did you feel the same way?

ROY: Pretty much the same.

US: How about after you'd calmed down following the bout you had with the TV repairman? How'd you feel then?

ROY: At first I felt great, then I thought maybe I'd lost my cool. My control. I don't know. I felt like a kid.

US: Then every time you lose your cool or your control you feel childish?

ROY: Yes.

US: Then maybe that's how some part of you *wants* to feel.

ROY: That's ridiculous.

US: Is it? You were doing very well for a while, and then you began slipping back. It's almost as if some part of you couldn't deal with being adult and taking full responsibility for handling conflict. The kid reasserted himself and you started losing control and losing your cool, and finally just losing. And right now you've put us in the role of playing your parents, telling you where you've gone wrong. *You* want to stop. You have to stay on top of the part of yourself that *doesn't.*

ROY: How?

US: First, recognize that part in you that is the childish little boy for what it is and then, when you feel him reasserting himself, grin, shrug, and say, "No, not this time."

ROY: I'll have a go at it.

Like most people, Roy started off with a complaint that had little to do with what was really bothering him: He told us our system didn't give people a chance to vent their anger. What he *really* wanted was for *us* to tell *him* how to *keep* from venting his anger! His mental equilibrium was dependent on his central belief that he was a child, and a bad child at that. So each time he began to behave in an adult, responsible manner, his balance was threatened. The child would simply have to learn that Roy was a worthwhile, valuable, mature person who didn't need a six-year-old subconscious to tell him he was a loser.

That's what we mean when we say *want.* We all *want* to stop smoking, but we create elaborate rationales to protect us from that change. We all *want* to stop losing, we all *want* to stop being a bully, but change is threatening to our behavior patterns. We'll have to accept some unpleasant truths about ourselves along the way. We'll have to acknowledge that some problems will always be with us. But, finally, we'll start grinning with confidence as we learn to stay on top of those problems.

FIRST YOU NEED A PLAN

One of the most sensible, structured ways we've found to design a plan comes from theater practice, from a method attributed to Konstantin Stanislavski, the great Russian teacher and director. In his method there are three points to deal with:

1. Objective: what you want
2. Obstacle: why you can't have it
3. Action: what you do to get it

On a piece of paper, write down the heading "Objectives." These are going to be your *wants*. ("Want" is a funny word. It works best when you express it positively: "I want to be pleasant" or "I want a plum." Turning that around, how do you not-want something? Does that mean you want something which happens to be nothing?)

Anyway, if change is what you seek in the area of your personal conflicts, write down three wants/objectives for yourself. Be careful to state them in a positive form. For example, instead of saying "I don't want to be a loser any more," you might say "I want to feel good about myself in conflict situations." Let the list of your wants come out freely. Don't edit them. You might just surprise yourself with some of the things you really care about. If your list runs longer than three, that's fine.

Once you've established your objectives, head up another piece of paper with the word "Obstacles." Underneath, list as many things as you can which seem to keep you from achieving each of your three (or more) wants. For example:

Objective (Want): I want to feel good about myself.
      Obstacles: 1. I'm not sure I'm a very worthwhile person.
             2. People around me aren't supportive.
             3. I'm shy.
             4. I have a bad temper.

Carry through and write down as many obstacles as you can think of for each of your three objectives.

On a third piece of paper, underneath the heading "Actions," write down the things you must *do* to get each of your objectives past each of the obstacles you've noted. For example:

Objective: I want to feel good about myself.
Obstacle: I'm not sure I'm a very worthwhile person.
 Actions: 1. *Remind* myself I can do it.
2. *Behave* as if I were worthwhile.
3. *Focus* on my strong points.
4. *Congratulate* myself!
5. *Stay on top of* the "child" in me who "needs" to fail.
6. *Center* myself.

Again, these are only examples, but you'll notice that what's good about the "Actions" list is that it is expressed in verbs: *Remind, Behave, Focus, Center,* etc. In other words, your list for achieving change is expressed in things you can do, not in homilies, parables, or old saws such as "Handsome is as handsome does." Each of your final actions is designed to get you what you want no matter what the obstacles.

That's the hard part. Now you've got to do what you've said you must. Post your "Actions" list and remind yourself of the points on the list several times a day. Don't answer the phone or write a letter without making sure you've centered yourself and focused on the actions that will help you reach your goals.

CONCLUSION?

How can there be a conclusion to a lifelong process? No matter who you are, it's always a question of being aware, of staying centered and regaining that center when you lose it. Nobody is ever finished with his responsibility for being aware.

And, of course, if you don't really *want* to change, you won't. Like the kleptomaniac at the beginning of the chapter, you have to make a choice. You may be able to change with great ease, but you just might not wish to. We've met many people who paradoxically, feel "healthier" when they engage in knockdown conflict. They talk about *getting it out of their systems* and so forth. And we've met others who try to find out how much somebody really loves them by picking a fight. If their "opponent" fights back with great energy, that's love. Fritz Redl, the great child psychologist, has written about children to whom love is a real threat. They require conflict for stability.

We cannot buy that. We've made a different choice, and although we defend the rights of those who choose differently, we are committed to our vision of harmony. We suspect you are, too.

Deep down inside.

XII

Now You Try It

He who will not apply new remedies
must expect old evils.

—Francis Bacon

Before you run right out on the street and look for your
first attacker, it might be revealing for you to take a little test
on Attack-tics to see what you've learned.

What follows is a series of sample conflict situations. For
each one, decide on the best course of action to take, based
on your Attack-tics training. As we've said all along, there
is more than one "correct" way to handle a conflict. The
important thing is to make choices which are grounded on
fair assessments of *each* situation, and not to get carried
away by old habits and old fears.

At the end of the chapter you'll find our considered opinion on each conflict so you can compare your own responses
with ours. In each case we ask you to try to put yourself in
the shoes of the central character and make as careful a
judgment as you can.

CASE #1: SAM

Sam Blodgett, age fifty-two, divorced. Salesman for industrial hardware, income approximately $30,000 a year. Lives alone, dates occasionally, enjoys golf. A history buff.

Sam is on the road, making his rounds—he works by appointment only, because a single sale in his business can amount to as much as twenty thousand dollars—and at this moment he sits in the waiting room of a large manufacturing firm. Five other businessmen are also waiting to see various executives. Sam's client in this instance is Alan Hofstader, a forty-year-old man who enjoys his reputation for being outspoken. Hofstader's outspokenness could be construed as hostility as much as anything else.

Sam has been kept waiting in the busy room for close to twenty minutes when Hofstader finally comes out, and begins speaking in a voice loud enough for everyone else to hear:

HOFSTADER: Blodgett? You back peddling that second rate stuff again? Jesus, you've got your nerve! The last garbage we bought from you people was late coming, half the order was assbackwards, and your billing department tried to screw us out of three thousand bucks! Why the hell should I even let you in here!?

What would you do if you were Sam?
Remember:
1) Hofstader shows no signs of kidding, even though, to the best of Sam's knowledge, none of the charges is true.
2) Hofstader shows no signs of letting up, either.
3) This is an important client.
Setting up the situation geometrically should help you decide.

When you have you planned Sam's course of action, turn to page 218 for our view.

CASE #2: CHRISTINE

Christine Vogel, age twenty, single, a college student living in a dorm room with three other women. She has one steady boyfriend. She wants to be a writer.

It's two A.M., and Christine has just returned from a fairly traumatic date with Carl, her regular boyfriend. Carl brought up the same old thing about wanting to quit college and get married. Christine told him she had no intention of quitting and even less intention of getting married right away. Carl stalked off in a huff.

One of Christine's roommates, Barbara, is still up, writing a term paper. They sit together to have a cup of coffee, and Christine is just beginning to feel a bit better about herself and the world when Barbara, something of an acerbic type anyway, begins:

BARBARA: You know I've always cared the world about you, Chris, but I guess somebody's got to tell you something about yourself. You know, for all your perceptivity, you've got a real problem. I don't even think you know it. You're so goddamned holier-than-thou, nobody wants to hang out with you. I'm surprised Carl has put up with you this long!

What do you—as Christine—do?
Remember:
1) Up to now Barbara and Christine have gotten along fine.
2) Christine cares about Barbara's friendship.

Again, try to see it geometrically. Then turn to page 222 for our view.

CASE #3: MARTY

Marty Franchini, female, age twenty-eight, married for eight years, mother of three boys. She works as a receptionist at the local radio station.

Marty is up for a job as producer's assistant, a job which means more money, prestige, and creative possibilities. She is anxious and can't wait to find out if she got the job, only to discover that management has decided to hire from outside the organization. Marty learns that she isn't going to get the job because Benjie, one of the staff announcers, had told everybody she was an alcoholic. Up to this point Marty had always had a cordial "Hi, how are ya?" relationship with the older man. Benjie has wife problems and could possibly have a bottle problem himself. There's no reason Marty can think of for his behavior, but her source, a young announcer whose loyalty is unquestionable, is certain that Benjie has killed her chance for promotion.

What do you—as Marty—do?
Remember:
1) Benjie *might* have a serious problem.
2) Benjie and Marty must continue working together.
3) Marty really wanted that job!
Again, use your Attack-tics geometry to clarify what's going on. Our solution is on page 225.

CASE #4: CHUCK

Chuck Blinn, age nineteen, administrative assistant in the office of a large hospital.

Chuck's duties at the hospital encompass, more or less regularly, everything nobody else wants to do. He schedules space, seminars, meetings, in-service courses, and the like. It's a thankless task because of the complexities of the staff problems, financial problems, and space problems. When things go well somebody else takes the credit. When things go badly, Chuck Blinn becomes the office goat.

After six months on the job, Chuck is given the task of setting up a multifaceted conference for Operating Room nurses. It's a three-day conference with simultaneous seminars and workshops on all the various aspects of O.R. procedures and skills. Chuck is thwarted at every turn by administrators, doctors, and nurses who have more important things to do than help "the kid" arrange time slots and room availability.

On the second day of the conference Chuck is collared in the hall by a surgeon who is furious about the room he's been assigned: It's too small for the overflow, last-minute registration. Moreover, the surgeon claims he ordered a 16mm projector, though Chuck has no record or memory of ever being asked to provide audiovisual equipment for this doctor. The surgeon is hardly understanding:

SURGEON: Listen, kid, my time is too valuable to spend chasing all over the place because you're too damned inefficient to get the simplest things through your pinhead!

There is a small audience for this interchange—a few nurses, an administrator . . .

What do you—as Chuck—do?

Remember:

1) Chuck has no recollection of having been asked to do the task in question.

2) The surgeon is an important man on the hospital staff.

3) Chuck doesn't love his job, but he does want to keep it. He hopes it will lead to better things.

For our view, see page 229.

CASE #5: SKIP HANSEN

Skip and Elaine Hansen have just moved into a new neighborhood with their two children, ages eight and ten. Skip is thirty-six, Elaine thirty-four. Skip is a social worker, directing the local counseling center for young people. Elaine is a CPA.

One of the first things the Hansens noticed when they moved in was that their next-door neighbors were in the habit of letting their two large standard poodles run free. The dogs were generally friendly, but they had decided to include the Hansens' half acre as part of their territory. The Hansens have no pets because their younger child is highly allergic to animal hair of any kind.

After a week of stepping in the dog droppings on his own front lawn, Skip went to the neighbors and complained as nicely as he could. For a few days the dogs were chained, but then their owners went back to their old lax ways. Skip complained again and got the same lip service as before. Finally, in a rage, Skip called the local dog warden and had the two poodles impounded. At six that night the neighbor, Mr. Devereaux, shows up at the Hansen front door slightly drunk.

DEVEREAUX: Listen, you twerp, you owe me ten bucks! I hadda pay ten bucks to get my dogs back because you went and blew the whistle on them! I'll get my money outa you one way or the other!

What do you—as Skip Hansen—do?
Remember:
1) Skip had already complained about the dogs—nicely.
2) Skip and Elaine like where they live.
3) Mr. Devereaux is drunk with more than rage.
For our view, see page 232.

CASE STUDIES: OUR VIEW
CASE #1: SAM

Geometry, Stage #1

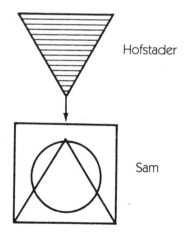

Hofstader

Sam

Stage #1: Hofstader attacks; Sam centers, keeping his options open, Doing Nothing until he makes a decision.

The tough thing for Sam Blodgett to do is to keep his center in the middle of this maelstrom. There was no way he could have known that Hofstader was going to come at him like that. The time and place belong to his angry client, and Sam will have to work hard to gain any advantage at all.

The fact that other people are present makes the situation doubly difficult to handle, for both men's egos are going to be involved: "I don't want to let all these people see me embarrassed" (Sam) and "I'm quite the showman and nobody puts one over on me" (Hofstader).

Then there's the element which underlies the whole transaction, namely that Hofstader may be off his nut but he's a big customer.

Sam Blodgett has the right to keep from being insulted in public. Nothing in his contract says he has to take abuse from neurotic clients unless, for some reason or other, he chooses to.

First in Sam's mind is to change things around and get Hofstader out of the driver's seat. He chooses Withdrawal (triangle) of a very specialized type. In the midst of Hofstader's harangue, leading from his center, Sam slips past the angry man and, without a word, goes through the door behind the receptionist and heads straight for Hofstader's private office.

Geometry, Stage #2

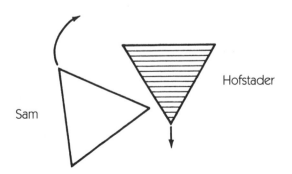

Sam

Hofstader

Sam's Withdrawal has the added element of surprise. Hofstader, left a bit mystified, is now forced to follow Sam back to his own office!

As soon as Hofstader arrives and they are alone, Sam nails him on the apex of his own triangle and Fights Back.

SAM: Look, Mr. Hofstader, I don't need to take that kind of abuse from you. We make a good product, and if you have problems with it you come right to me and I'll do my damndest to serve you. Now let's see if we can't deal with what's bothering you.

Geometry, Stage #3

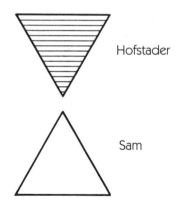

Hofstader

Sam

The effect of Fighting Back at the attacking Hofstader is enough to chasten the buyer, forcing him into the Parley mode, where both men can sit down and talk reasonably.

Geometry, Stage #4

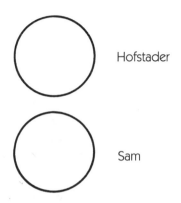

Hofstader

Sam

As we said, there are lots of other options, depending on your particular framing of the situation. You may have judged Hofstader's spirit as resolute and made a complete and final Withdrawal. Or you may have entered into Aiki right there in the waiting room—but in our opinion that would have been very risky. Hofstader was putting on a show, and it's hard to get anything resolved during a show.

Or you might have tried Deception. A friend of ours in a similar situation grabbed his chest and sank down on the couch, trying to look pale. The attacker, an insecure man anyway, was overcome with remorse for his stupidity, and even laughed when our friend said, "Christ, if it takes a heart attack to get *your* attention, I'd hate to go before your board of directors!" So much for Deception.

If you chose a square mode, deciding to wait out Hofstader while he ran himself down, that, too, would have been acceptable. But with the presence of an audience, Hofstader would soon have embarrassed himself. And that's not exactly keeping yourself in the protective spirit.

The only option we'll absolutely disallow you at this point is your getting into a point-by-point fight about whose hardware is better and whose billing department is flawless. Since this is not a win/lose situation, that would be a fight strictly for ego.

CASE #2: CHRISTINE

Geometry, Stage #1

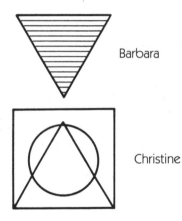

Barbara

Christine

Stage #1: Barbara attacks; Christine centers, keeping her options open, Doing Nothing until she chooses.

The time is wrong, the timing is wrong, and Barbara has the advantage of surprise as well. Who wants to discuss personality flaws at two in the morning? Especially after you've been arguing all night with your lover! Christine could run off to her bedroom, slam the door, and make Barbara feel a little bit guilty, but she wouldn't accomplish much. And it certainly wouldn't help her get to sleep.

Christine could stand square and let Barbara do her worst, but that might make Barbara try all the harder to drag her into the melee.

Christine could point her triangle straight at Barbara and Fight Back: "I don't care what you think! Who appointed you expert?" But that would probably give Barbara just the response she is looking for.

The best of the choices appears to us to be a combination of Aiki and Deception: "You're right, Barbara." It's almost Aiki except that Christine doesn't really believe that Barbara is right. But at two A.M., who cares? If Barbara *is* right, Christine might learn something; if she's wrong, she's wrong. But the response Barbara is least prepared for is to have Christine say *without irony,* "Yes, you're right." Besides, there is no winner or loser in a situation like this.

Geometry, Stage #2

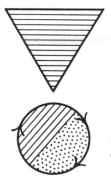

Barbara

Christine
(Deception + Aiki)

Barbara is caught off balance and is now stuck with having to fill in the blanks in the conversation: "Well . . . uh, what are you going to do about it?" she stammers. Christine replies, "I don't know."

With any luck Barbara will begin to feel very awkward about the whole matter. Christine is not feeding her anything to work with, and Barbara may even realize that she's way off base, that what she said isn't completely true.

More often than not—if the attacker is a reasonable person —the attacker will begin backing and filling, turning more and more circular: "Really you're not all that bad. Maybe I kind of overreacted . . ."

Geometry, Stage #3

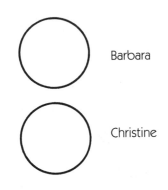

Barbara

Christine

Christine has allowed Barbara the opportunity to confront her own aggression. That's the favor Christine is doing her roommate, so long as she remembers to stay centered even while her feelings are being hurt.

CASE #3: MARTY

Geometry, Stage #1

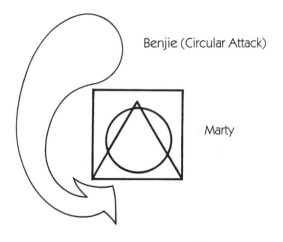

Benjie (Circular Attack)

Marty

Stage #1: Benjie attacks circularly while Marty remains centered, Doing Nothing until she can proceed.

Benjie's is the classic circular attack. It's off balance, completely unexpected, and devastating in its impact on the target. Marty really was losing out on an important job because of Benjie's smear campaign.

The importance of this event makes it doubly difficult for Marty to hang on to any last shreds of her balanced approach. Benjie has virtually taken food out of her and her children's mouths.

First she moves in on Benjie in a triangular mode, only to find when she confronts him with her charges that he disavows any knowledge of them whatsoever. His façade is impenetrable. Short of getting him on sodium pentothal, there seems to be very little chance of forcing him to confess.

Geometry, Stage #2

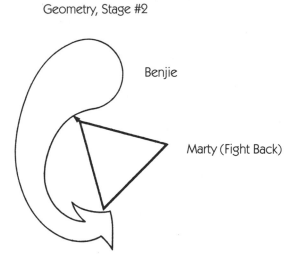

Benjie

Marty (Fight Back)

If this were not so important an issue, Marty might be justified in going back to the square mode, Doing Nothing, and waiting the situation out. Instead, she makes an appointment with her boss (who's also involved in this) and, continuing in the triangular mode, lays out her understanding of what's happened. Then she asks her boss to arrange a meeting that will include all three of them: Marty, her boss, and Benjie. All the way along the line, Marty is on balance, coming from her center, seeking to restore harmony and truth.

Geometry, Stage #3

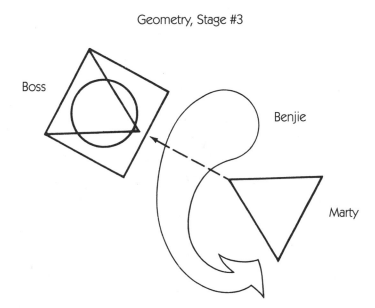

At the confrontation, Marty aims her triangle directly through Benjie to the boss, and Benjie realizes he can't dodge any further. The boss knows where he first heard about Marty's drinking problem, and now he wishes he hadn't taken Benjie's word for it. (In a way, Marty's boss was a party to Benjie's circular attack by not dealing on the line with Marty earlier.)

As soon as Benjie confesses, Marty can switch into the circular mode:

MARTY: Look, Benjie, I know life's difficult sometimes, and I know you were nervous about working with a woman. Let's try to figure out a way we can function together.

Geometry, Stage #4

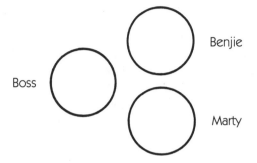

All three persons are now in the Parley mode.

Within a month Marty occupied the job as producer's assistant, and she and Benjie were able to work in harmony. We'll grant you that Marty's tack took guts and an incredible amount of self-control, but it was by no means an impossible feat. Every one of us, no matter what our character structure, can do the same. Moreover, we owe it to our attackers to help them return to balance before they hurt someone else, themselves, or us. Remember: You do no one a favor by letting an important issue go unresolved.

CASE #4: CHUCK

Geometry, Stage #1

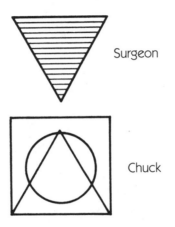

Surgeon

Chuck

Stage #1: The surgeon attacks; Chuck centers himself, Doing Nothing until he selects his option.

Perhaps the most important thing here is that Chuck is dealing not with an isolated event but with a long-standing problem: He is given no support and has fallen into the role of "goat" for any problems which come up. It might be different if he were incompetent, but that is plainly not the case. It is important that he get out from under this role. To do this, he'll have to make a public, dramatic break. So, turning the situation to his advantage, Chuck chooses to Fight Back.

Geometry, Stage #2

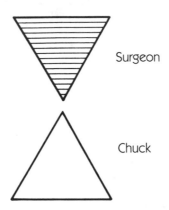

Surgeon

Chuck

Had Chuck chosen to Do Nothing and taken the abuse, nothing of a permanent nature would have been achieved. Had he chosen Deception or Parley, again, nothing would have been altered in the basic structure of his job. Chuck realized he'd have to risk everything in order to change everything:

CHUCK: Listen, Doctor, I won't be insulted because you're angry at the situation. I'm angry too, but I'm angry because I've had to organize this entire conference without any help from you, the administration, the participants, or anyone else here! As for your room assignment, that was a result of late registrations. What's more, I have no record of your request for a projector because you never got around to filling out the form! Now, you can stay on my back or you can try to solve the problem with me.

SURGEON: I don't have to take this from you!

CHUCK: If you want to stop me, get off my case and figure out which room you want. You switch rooms, and I'll see if I can get you a projector.

With that Chuck kept his center and made a fast exit, leaving the surgeon with the job of either continuing his recriminations or doing something with his overflow crowd.

Geometry, Stage #3

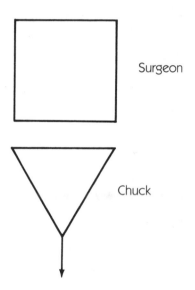

Surgeon

Chuck

Chuck Withdraws after his attack, leaving the surgeon standing squarely in the middle of the hall.

Chuck wisely forced his attacker to focus on the problem and its solution. Then, after venting his anger in a reasonable manner and saying what he felt he had to say, Chuck withdrew. If he loses his job over this incident, well, he had no intention of continuing under these conditions anyway. More likely, he'll keep his job and conditions will improve for him. Conflict *can* make things better if we have the nerve to enter into it in a clearheaded, balanced way. Of course, we should know up-front what we are risking.

CASE #5: SKIP HANSEN

Geometry, Stage #1

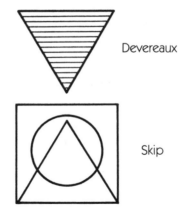

Devereaux

Skip

Stage #1: Mr. Devereaux attacks as Skip Hansen preserves his options.

The episode with the dogs is as close to a violent conflict as any we've seen. Mr. Devereaux is clearly ready to do battle over ten dollars and his neighbor's treachery in calling the dog warden. He threatens violence if he doesn't get his pride and his ten bucks back.

In the actual event from which this case study is derived,

the conflict never reached physical expression because Skip
handled it so well. He kept his center even though Devereaux
was substantially larger than he was.

SKIP: I sure don't blame you for getting sore, Come on in.

Geometry, Stage #2

Devereaux

Skip

In this instance Skip made an open, Aiki response. He then
shifted gears only slightly to turn and invite Devereaux to
enter. He made a good move and walked away from Devereaux to let the man follow him inside. By offering his back
Skip was saying two things, both of which exerted a calming
influence on the angry neighbor: "I'm not afraid" and "I'm
not going to fight you, so *you* don't have to be afraid."

Devereaux was caught off balance by Skip's warm behavior
and, instead of focusing on his objective, began to feel vaguely
cheated.

DEVEREAUX: Listen, Hansen, you had no right to go and
call the cops on my dogs. You shoulda come
to me first.

SKIP: I guess I really must have been exasperated.

DEVEREAUX: Hunh?

SKIP: I must have really felt upset to do something that drastic. Like calling the dog warden.

DEVEREAUX: Why'd you do it?

SKIP: I was very upset.

DEVEREAUX: How come?

Notice that Skip has maneuvered the situation so that Devereaux is now at least trying to look in the same direction as Skip. They are in harmony of a sort, able to Parley, both examining Skip's feelings and his reason for calling the dog pound.

SKIP: I don't know. Maybe my feelings were hurt because you hadn't paid any attention to me?

DEVEREAUX: What!

SKIP: Well, I'd talked to you a couple of times about your trying to keep your dogs on your lawn, and there they were traipsing across my lawn again and again. It made me feel small. Like nothing I say or do has any effect at all.

Geometry, Stage #3

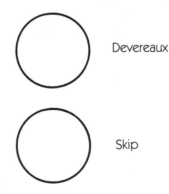

Devereaux

Skip

At this point, Skip has maneuvered Devereaux into a Parley. It's been gradual, but as soon as Devereaux begins to deal with the *mutual* problem of neighboring, he's a circle. Then, in the fourth stage, true confluence takes over.

DEVEREAUX: It's not like that at all . . . I mean, it's no big thing. We just forget. But it doesn't have anything to do with you . . .

SKIP: Yeah, I guess. But what should I do?

DEVEREAUX: Call me. I'm sorry they bug you so much. We don't mean anything by it. You kinda forget, that's all.

SKIP: Yeah, I can understand that.

DEVEREAUX: I just didn't know they bugged you that much. I'm really sorry.

SKIP: Me too.

Geometry, Stage #4

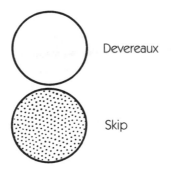

Devereaux

Skip

Aiki Confluence

Aiki confluence. Now the two "combatants" can experience the harmony as they try to deal on the same line, walk around in each other's skin. Devereaux, like so many of his brothers and sisters, had no idea that his actions had any real impact on anybody else. Skip gave him a real gift: the gift of knowing that he counted for something—even negatively. Not only was the attack defused, but the whole dog situation was brought under control.

There's no way to score how well you did on these sample conflicts. We can't say that three "right" out of five gives you a passing grade. There are no right or wrong answers. What is important is that you have begun to make selections based on your own assessment of the conflict situation rather than reacting out of the passion of the moment, win/lose theories, or old bits of childhood behavior which have stuck with you.

The true test of your progress in Attack-tics will, of course, be in your own lives.

XIII

The Most Hostile
Aggressor of All

It isn't a communist or a fascist, a Ku Kluxer, a psycho-path, or a hit man from the mob.

The aggressor is you.

The victim is a good, worthwhile person who deserves the very best at everyone's hands. The victim has every right to walk through life without being hurt by you.

The victim is you.

Every day there are billions of internal "muggings" and suicidal attacks on one's soul which go unpunished and un-resolved.

In an average day most human beings seem to attack themselves at least once an hour. "You fool, what'd you say that for?" "You turkey! Who told you you knew how to play tennis?" "You jerk! When are you gonna grow up?" The voice of the attacker belongs to us as we speak to ourselves, berating and belittling our own efforts, thoughts, abilities, physiques, talents, faces, skin tone, and any other thing we can get hold of.

And the attacker is relentless. We are probably harder on ourselves than we are on any of our friends. The attacker is shameless. He or she doesn't know the definition of "kind." The attacker just keeps pushing us further and further away from the image of ourselves as good, competent human beings.

It doesn't much matter how we came to this sorry pass—whether our mothers were strong and our fathers weak or vice versa—we are there and we don't have to be.

If Attack-tics works when you're attacked by someone else, it ought to work equally well if the attacker is you and the victim is your own self-esteem. A bully is a bully and off balance is off balance and aggression is aggression. It may mean you'll have to do some serious talking to yourself—hold some long conversations—but it'll be worth it in the long run, believe us.

Most self-inflicted attacks follow the same geometric pattern as external attacks. The attacking self is usually triangular and aimed right at your core, your heart, your center, your spirit, that "part" of you which is in charge of feeling good about yourself. Recent studies indicate that while these attacks are not physical, they can have physical manifestations. For example, if you keep telling yourself you're clumsy, sure as raisins have wrinkles, you'll trip at every opportunity. Or try shooting a basket while you tell yourself over and over again "I can't do it, I can't do it . . ." You'll be lucky if the ball even touches the rim. One experiment we're especially fond of is asking people to walk forward while thinking backward. Try it. Walk along at your normal gait but imagine at the same time that you're going in the opposite direction.

Too many of us do exactly that without knowing it.

Well, if the geometry is the same, then the responses should work out pretty much the same way too. We can Fight Back, Withdraw, Parley, Do Nothing, Deceive, or become confluent with our attacking selves. All we need do is assess the spirit of the attack and then respond.

FIGHTING YOURSELF

Let's suppose you're about to go into an important meeting and the critical voice begins telling you that you're not suited for the job, your personal appearance is all wrong, they won't like you, and so on. You center yourself, become a triangle, and deal right on that line:

"Listen, friend, I'm in no mood to fool around with your criticisms today. I'm only going to tell you once: Don't mess with me."

If your attacker is very strong-willed, you may have to shift gears, but that's okay too. If, after you've read him or her the riot act, your attacking self keeps up the negative flow, you will have to try another mode.

WITHDRAWING FROM YOURSELF

Every day people run away from themselves; in this instance, however, we're asking that you raise your use of Withdrawal to a conscious level and use it only for very specific purposes.

Let's say you're doing some intricate work: embroidery, carpentry, anything which takes your full concentration. Your attacker begins to shove you around: "You're gonna goof! . . . Watch it! . . . You never were very good with your hands, were you! . . . Gee, all that work and it's still gonna look lousy . . . Just like all the other lousy work you've done before . . ." Certainly, you could go head-to-head with your attacker, as in the previous example: "Listen, voice, you better shut up and leave me alone!" Or, still remaining triangular, you could point your apex of energy, resources, and intention in a different direction—in effect, Withdrawing from the conflict.

For example, you're working on the embroidery and the attack begins:

"You're gonna goof! Watch it!"

You take a moment, center, and redirect your focus of concentration (the pointy end of the triangle) as sharply as you can on your task. It's not that you pay no attention to your inner critic; rather, you're so preoccupied with your job that you have no room for the ranting and raving of the negative voice.

You do it consciously and you do it from your center.

PARLEYING WITH YOURSELF

You have discussions with yourself all the time. Why not formalize these episodes and enter into the spirit of compromise?

> YOU #1: You're doing it again. You're making another one of those dumb decisions you always make so badly.
>
> YOU #2: What would you do?
>
> YOU #1: I wouldn't call her up so soon after the first date, that's what I wouldn't do.
>
> YOU #2: Okay, what *would* you do?
>
> YOU #1: I'd let her think I wasn't too anxious.
>
> YOU #2: Isn't that dishonest?
>
> YOU #1: I'd rather be dishonest than have everybody think I couldn't get a date.
>
> YOU #2: I'm not so sure. How come I can't act the way I feel?
>
> YOU #1: Because she'll misunderstand.
>
> YOU #2: Then I'll make it clearer for her. [And so on . . .]

The Parley turned out to be a good one, with both sides of the personality getting a fair hearing. Notice that You #2 played it very low-key, listened, and learned some things. By not Fighting Back, he was able to get You #1 to behave rationally and make his points in a reasonable manner. You #2 was willing to compromise, and his spirit was clearly open to change. That choice resulted in a much more organic dialogue than any fight would have produced.

Again, simply follow the rules for Parley and talk to yourself.

DOING NOTHING

"Hey, dummy! With a face like yours it's a wonder anybody'd ever marry you! Hey, ugly!"

Doing Nothing can be a highly effective means of getting your attacking self to give up. As the voice goes on and on, you get hold of your center, waiting out the long stream of counterproductive garbage until your attacker gets bored and quits. It takes a relaxed smile, a lot of patience, and a strong grip on your center, but it works wonders. Know inside yourself that you aren't one tenth as awful as your attacker says you are. Know that you're a dynamite person and that you can survive all the puerile attacks your inner voice visits on you.

DECEIVING YOURSELF

Self-deception hardly requires any introduction. We do it all the time and with great ease. For many of us the only

thing that keeps us going is our ability to deceive ourselves
into thinking that everything's fine.

But we're not talking about *that* kind of self-deception.
We're talking about the kind that is consciously applied. The
kind where you know you're doing it and you know why
you're doing it. You're choosing Deception in the circular
mode as a means of solving some inner conflict.

You will probably need a little more imagination and a
little more of a sense of humor to employ this mode on
yourself, because you know yourself so well. But, used correctly, it can still work for you.

Imagine that you're sitting alone in your living room after
having just put your children to bed with about a 9.9 degree
of difficulty. The attacking voice begins to poke you where
you live: your ability (or lack of it) as a parent.

> YOU #1: Well, you sure as hell blew that one, didn't you? I
> thought you said you weren't going to make the
> same mistakes your parents made with you. You
> sounded just like your mother, for Christ's sake! I
> tell you, your kids are going to grow up to be really
> screwed up after you're finished with them!

Instead of Fighting Back or running away or Doing Nothing or rolling over and playing dead, YOU #2 responds.

> YOU #2: I think I'll be worse than my mother. I mean, if
> I'm already so rotten, why not go with the flow
> here? Tomorrow I'll tie them up and lock them in
> the cellar. Then I'll start the whipping part. Right
> now I'm only a spanker. With luck I could develop
> into a first-rate whipper.
> YOU #1: I'm not kidding!
> YOU #2: Neither am I. I really am going to do all those
> marvelous things.

YOU #1: You're crazy.

YOU #2: No crazier than a voice who never tells me anything supportive, who never says anything about the good things I've done.

YOU #1: I'll deal with you later!

YOU #2: Don't forget to write!

A bizarre way to treat yourself, perhaps, but it still does the job. Sometimes you just have to kid yourself a bit to remind yourself that "Hey, goddammit, you're really a terrific person!"

The hard part is to remember that there are *two* voices in there, not just the voice of doom. Once you nonclinically split your personality, all inner conflicts can be handled if you get together with your centered, positive self. And smile!

AIKING YOURSELF

It's nicest, of course, when you can flow with yourself. You can't always do that, Lord knows, but you can look for more and more opportunities than you're currently finding. We all can.

Aiki, as you remember, is circular, an entering into and joining with the force of the off-balance attacker who's threatening to demolish you. It's no different if the attacker is an inner self who claims to have an inside track on truth, beauty, and goodness. To Aiki yourself, you simply give up the impulse to struggle with the attacking force and join it, harmonize with it as you lead it to a safe position for both of you.

For example, let's say you are busily damning yourself for not coming to the aid of your closest friend:

YOU #1: You should have done something when you saw Jay screaming at Diane. You could have come to her aid, but you were too goddamned chicken. You were afraid Jay would turn on you, weren't you?

YOU #2: Could you tell me what this is all about?

YOU #1: You heard me. I called you a chicken. A coward!

YOU #2: I know. I just wondered why, is all.

YOU #1: Because you are.

YOU #2: Why does that hurt you so much?

YOU #1: I don't like cowards. I don't like you.

YOU #2: How does it feel?

YOU #1: Crummy.

YOU #2: I don't blame you for hating me, then. I guess the next time one of those kind of situations comes up, I should let *you* take over.

YOU #1: You're right. I should.

YOU #2: What would *you* have done?

YOU #1: I would have told Jay to leave Diane alone and stop being so hard on her.

YOU #2: What do you think would have happened?

YOU #1: He would have stopped.

YOU #2: Then what?

YOU #1: I don't know. I guess Jay would have told me to mind my own business.

YOU #2: That's not so bad. How would Diane have felt?

YOU #1: I don't know.

YOU #2: Did she ask for help?

YOU #1: Of course not. She's too proud.

YOU #2: What would your helping have done, then?

YOU #1: (Pause.) Well ... but I still think you're a chicken.

YOU #2: I don't blame you. It must be hard understanding me.

YOU #1: Nothing's really easy, is it?

YOU #2: No, but we do pretty well for ourself.

YOU #1: Yeah ... I guess we do ...

Pollyannaish? We don't think so. Not if the result is harmony. Not if a nice kind of inner ease settles down over the two warring factions within you. Certainly it's tough to maintain that balance. The attacking voice will start up again as soon as you make another mistake—for you will make more mistakes—and then you'll have to make another choice between the three shapes and the six responses to conflict. But our experience shows us that the more you deal on the line with yourself and the more centered you become, the less you'll have to spend huge fractions of your days locked in combat with yourself. Soon it will become second nature to you. The voice will say "jerk-idiot-dummy" and you'll click right into a response that feels right for the situation:

"Yeah, I guess you're right, but do you have any idea how hard it is to be a jerk-idiot-dummy?"

The wages of harmony are peace. Inside with yourself, outside with everyone else. In some ways it's harder to work to treat yourself right than it is to give in to all the rotten thoughts you have about yourself. But it's the kind of effort we feel is well worth making.

XIV

The Spirit of Attack-tics and the Attack-tics of Spirit

> The world's battlefields are in the heart.
>
> —Henry Ward Beecher

Throughout the book we've used the expression "protective spirit."

Just what is this spirit that is so protective? What is it designed to protect?

To answer either of these questions it's necessary to return to the concept of centering. By this point you should be fairly conversant with your own center. You should have begun to experience the sensations which accompany your return to balance. You should be equally familiar with what it feels like to lose your center, to be off balance. For most people it divides along these lines:

UNCENTERED	CENTERED
off balance	*balanced*
asleep	*aware*
hysterical	*calm*

scattered	focused
tense	relaxed
projective	intuitive
paranoid	realistic
split	whole

Needless to say, it's a pretty loaded list. It's loaded because the uncentered person has lost contact with himself as an organic whole which is part of a larger whole with which he is connected. *Spirit has to do with that sense of connection.*

As we said earlier, your center connects you to yourself in time and space; it is the nexus, the junction box, if you will. Experiencing your center makes questions about mind versus body unnecessary. Mind and body are one at that intersection of center.

But your center connects you to more than yourself; it is the center of relationships between you and every other thing in the world. Deny that receptor and you cut yourself off from those relationships. So the protective spirit has to do with that indissoluble connection between your center and the centers of even the most difficult-to-like of your acquaintances.

Many people who are new to the martial arts labor under the fantasy that when they get proficient they will be able to "really kick ass." Likewise, many who begin psychotherapy imagine that "cured" means they'll be able to boss people around. Having spent much of their lives afraid to assert themselves to "get what they want," they imagine that their new power will give them the nerve or self-confidence to get back at all the people and situations which have made them feel small all these years. They carry with them a great deal of anger which they cannot release, and it is this anger which directs their fantasy of revenge.

What they don't realize is that it is really their lack of connection to themselves that prevents them from functioning well. If their training in martial arts, or their therapy, is "successful," they appear quite different from their original fantasy. Having found their spirit and experienced their energy, they never quite get around to "kicking ass." The need for revenge is gone because *their reconnection with their own centers has put them back into connection with all life.* The protective spirit has to do with that union of life with life.

Spirit is also rooted in the present, a function of the intersection of time with your own energy. Spirit is not Then or Soon; spirit is Right This Minute. You can't save spirit or reflect on it, because it is like Thales' moving stream. You cannot step in the same water twice. The molecules that are here now are gone by the time you finish reading this sentence.

To illustrate the nowness of spirit there's a tale which tells of a Zen master who, when a section of ground gave way beneath his feet, found himself clinging to the side of a cliff, holding on to a slim branch which began to crack under his weight. A few inches away he spotted the most beautiful strawberry he'd ever seen, and his concentration was riveted on the loveliness of this luscious fruit. His handhold was cracking, but it would break later. He lived in the now.

It's not our intention to have you fall off a cliff while you're preoccupied with strawberries, but all of us could begin to observe our spirit, our centeredness, our attitude and focus, to sharpen it and keep it in the now. Spirit has to do with what is happening now, not with worrying about what can happen or could happen or might happen.

Spirit is also energy—not necessarily the energy which you need to get up out of your chair and go look in the refrigerator (it includes that kind, too), but the energy which galvanizes you, courses through you, keeps you going, makes you despondent or joyous, well or sick, electrifies your curiosity, supports your emotions, gives you "charisma," makes your skin glow, focuses your life or disperses it, makes you clear in your heart, creates warmth or coolness, and melts with another energy in the act of making love. It is what makes you vital.

The spirit we speak of, then, when we talk of the protective spirit is 1) your center, 2) your connection to all life, time, and space, 3) nowness, and 4) energy. It protects you not because you are you but because you are alive; it protects the lives of others not because they are good friends of yours but because they are alive as well.

The Japanese call this protective spirit *ki,* a word which is almost untranslatable—we certainly have no other word which encompasses everything we've said about spirit so far. The Japanese language reflects the central importance of this word, for there are literally hundreds of words which include the syllable *ki* to denote the ever-present role of this elusive concept. Loosely translated, when you are sick, you have "bad" *ki;* when you are what we call insane, you have "different" *ki.* Most feelings, states, attitudes, and approaches to life are comprehensible to the Japanese through the concept of *ki.*

In a very real way, then, the goal of Attack-tics is the development of *ki,* not to learn a process just so you can go out and do battle—just as the ability to break boards with your feet is not the ultimate goal of karate.

After all, what is the significance of handling aggression? Have you invested all this time in practicing Attack-tics so that you can devastate your boss? Is your only goal the development of something which, for lack of a better term, you call "self-confidence"?

The pursuit of wholeness is what Attack-tics is really

about—to help you end that gnawing sense that parts of you are missing, that you aren't finished, that everybody else has something you lack.

How many times have you ordered something—a car, a dress, a new house, a boat, a TV set—convinced that this thing would make you really happy, make you feel complete? And then the thing arrived. Your excitement was every bit as great as you dreamed it would be. You drove the thing or wore the thing or sailed it or turned it on—and then, not long afterward, a strange, unsettling sense of disappointment overcame you.

It was the thing you ordered, but it wasn't as perfect as you thought it would be.

It was the thing you ordered, but it wasn't as fulfilling as you thought it would be.

It was the thing you ordered, but you got bored with it faster than you'd thought you would.

So you went back to dreaming. Maybe if you had ordered something else? Maybe a Porsche 912 with quad stereo and a quartz dash clock? Perhaps that would have made you as happy as you have every right to be?

We all know that a new hobby is not going to fill us up, that a new suit is not going to make us whole. But that awareness doesn't seem to count for much when we're feeling empty. It's worth a try, we say, and off we go to the shopping center.

Whole is what we want.

Whole is who we were a long long time ago. Before the pains came: the pain of growing up, the pain of being told we couldn't do it, the pain of flunking, the pain of hearing that our bodies were nasty, the pain of repeated failure, repeated stupidity, repeated punishment. It didn't take us long to learn that we could make up for our smallness by yelling louder or hitting harder. Or we learned that we could justify our bad feelings about ourselves by living down to our expectations—and failing.

Bully or chicken, winner or loser, victimizer or victim, we all want to be whole. It's just that we take different roads.

And we feel vaguely cheated when none of them leads to wholeness. To quote the old phrase, "You can't get there from here."

Spirit, *ki* the protective spirit, the spirit of Attack-tics, is all one thing: the act of putting the pieces back where they belong. It's the act of reestablishing contact with ourselves. It's the act of making ourselves whole again.

We said at the very outset of this book that a reader *could* practice Attack-tics in a manipulative manner. It is possible for a liar or a cheat to use Aiki or any of the other five attack responses and aim for a "kill" or a "win" over somebody who has made the mistake of attacking him.

But a strange thing begins to happen to people who become involved with Attack-tics, even if it's for the wrong reasons. The repeated practice of centering, of balancing, of flowing with an opponent causes a gradual change in the person doing the centering, balancing, and flowing with. It may be subtle at first, but even the most mean-spirited of people begin to relinquish their grasp on their aggression, lose their anger, and reconnect with the living force. Either that or they throw the system over and return to their old ways of handling attacks.

We'll take the leap of faith and assume you're not mean-spirited, that you *do* want to be whole. Be aware that you're embarking on a trip that is bigger and better than mere conflict-management skills. You'll have those as well, but you'll also start to perceive how you fit into the natural scheme of things. You'll spend less time feeling separate from the rest of the world, and less time feeling separate from yourself.

And that's not to say it will be easy. Almost half the events, people, and institutions in your life will be erecting barriers in your way. There will be constant tugs urging you to return to the "good old days" when you threw angry fits every week and went on crying jags. Changes in your behavior may be threatening to those closest to you. They may say they want you different, but when you start acting differently they become anxious about where they stand. They're forced to question their own behavior, and they may not be ready to do that.

You'll have to protect them even while they're trying to drag you down. It's not the protective spirit to laud your gorgeous new personality over anyone.

That doesn't mean that you have to go along on their ride, either. Keep your center and you'll know which way you have to go. Help others find theirs.

We have no terrific anecdote to end with. Nothing designed to "prove" you bought the right book. All we want you to know, from our heart to yours—along the shortest and most direct line that connects us—is that as part of the Living you are beautiful. As part of the Living you have the *right* to protect yourself. As part of the Living you have the *duty* to protect others.

Keep your centers. We love you.

Attack-tics Reminders

FOR YOUR REFRIGERATOR DOOR

Post them, refer to them, remember them.

LOSS IS NOT NECESSARILY DEFEAT

1. THERE'S NOTHING WRONG WITH WINNING, PROVIDED THAT WHAT YOU ARE WINNING IS A CONTEST

   NOT ALL CONFLICTS ARE CONTESTS

2. WHAT'S THE BEST/WORST THING THAT COULD HAPPEN TO ME/HIM IF I/HE WINS/LOSES?

3. CONFLICT IS PART OF THE NATURAL ORDER OF THINGS

   ALL CONFLICTS ARE NOT EQUALLY THREATENING

   ALL CONFLICTS ARE NOT EQUALLY SERIOUS

   BE AWARE OF YOUR CONFLICTS

4. THE SIX BASIC CONFLICT OPTIONS ARE:
   FIGHTING BACK
   WITHDRAWAL
   PARLEY
   DOING NOTHING
   DECEPTION
   AIKI

   NOT ALL PRINCIPLE IS SERIOUS PRIORITY

YOU HAVE THE RIGHT TO LIFE AND THE SANCTION OF THE UNIVERSE TO FIGHT TO PRESERVE IT

DON'T FIGHT TO PRESERVE IT

DON'T FIGHT IF YOU DON'T HAVE TO

NEVER FIGHT ANYONE WHO HAS NOTHING TO LOSE

ALWAYS RESPOND FROM YOUR CENTER

USE THE MINIMUM FORCE NECESSARY TO RESTORE HARMONY

IN ANY CONFLICT YOU MUST ESTIMATE:
    PERTINENCE
    TIME
    PLACE
    SPIRIT

FIGHT BACK IN THREE STAGES:
    IMMOBILIZATION
    CONTROL
    RESTORATION OF HARMONY

UNFAIR FIGHTING CAUSES YOUR OPPONENT TO FIGHT HARDER

GENERALIZATIONS AND EXAGGERATIONS MAKE IT DIFFICULT TO CONTROL THE OPPOSITION

5. THE PURPOSE OF CONFLICT IS HARMONY

6. THE BEST VICTORY IS THE ONE IN WHICH EVERYBODY WINS

YOUR BODY COMMUNICATES YOUR INTENTIONS THROUGH:
    FACE

POSTURE (INCLUDING HANDS AND
ARMS)
SPATIAL RELATIONSHIP

ATTACK WHEN IT IS A QUESTION OF LIFE OR
DEATH

WHEN THERE IS NO OTHER OPTION

WHEN IT IS A QUESTION OF SERIOUS PRIORITY

IT ALL CENTERS AROUND BALANCE

IT ALL BALANCES AROUND CENTER

AIKI: ACCEPT, HARMONIZE, REDIRECT, LEAD

BE THE WATER, NOT THE ROCK

CIRCULAR ATTACKS ARE DESIGNED TO:
    DECEIVE
    CONFUSE
    BUY TIME

ALL ENEMIES ARE BAD ENEMIES

THE MORE COMMITTED YOUR ATTACKER IS,
THE EASIER IT IS FOR YOU TO HANDLE HIM IF
YOU'RE BALANCED

THE WAGES OF HARMONY ARE PEACE

SPIRIT IS THE UNION OF LIFE WITH LIFE

WHOLE IS WHAT WE WANT

YOU DO NO ONE A FAVOR BY LETTING A
CONFLICT GO UNRESOLVED

7. THE SHORTEST DISTANCE BETWEEN YOU AND
ANYTHING ELSE IS A STRAIGHT LINE

CONTROL YOUR EMOTIONS

KNOW WHICH SHAPE PREDOMINATES AND USE
IT IN THE PROTECTIVE SPIRIT

8. FIRE   EARTH   WATER
ATTACK DOING NOTHING DECEPTION
WITHDRAWAL   PARLEY
                          AIKI

9. TAKE CARE OF YOURSELF BECAUSE YOU DESERVE IT

Terry Dobson

Terry Dobson studied in Japan for ten years with the founder of aikido, Morihei Ueshiba. Before his death in late 1992, he had taught aikido for twenty-five years and brought its principles to conflict management and personal growth seminars in education, mediation and business. In recent years he worked in the men's movement, giving seminars with Robert Bly, James Hillman and Jack Kornfield.

Victor Miller is a television and film writer living in Milford, Connecticut. He wrote the original script for *Friday the 13th* and writes for television daytime drama series.